ABOUT THE AUTHOR

Jennifer Manson is a writer and business woman. She lives in Brittany with her husband, teenage daughter and two cats. She is the author of six novels: *The Moment of Change*, *Tasha Stuart interviews ...*, *The Old Occidental Writers' Hotel*, *Law of Attraction*, *Slow Time* and *Inventor*.

For six years she was also a regular contributor to the "at home" supplement of the *Press* newspaper in New Zealand.

Jennifer is The Flow Writer, working with speakers and other experts to write their books.

Easy – Stories from an effortlessly created life is her first full-length, personal non-fiction work.

Easy

Stories from an effortlessly created life

Jennifer Manson

First published in France in 2013

Copyright © Jennifer Manson 2013

The moral right of the author has been asserted.

All rights reserved.

No part of this publication may be reproduced, stored in a retrieval system, or transmitted, in any form or by any means, without the prior permission in writing of the author, nor be otherwise circulated in any form of binding or cover other than that in which it is published and without a similar condition including this condition being imposed on the subsequent purchaser.

ISBN 978-0-473-25482-7

Cover design by Mega Advertising Ltd, NZ

www.jennifermanson.co.nz and
www.theflowwriter.com

ACKNOWLEDGEMENTS

To my daughter, Alex, my son, Jono, and my wonderful husband, Paul;

To my beautifully encouraging editor, Tanya Tremewan;

To my writing buddy, poet Kerrin P. Sharpe, who accompanied me on the journey from aspiring to actual;

To my publicist, Katie Read, for sending me out into the world farther than I would think to go myself;

To my brilliant coaches and mentors: Saskia Clements, Dave Kibby and Lucy Whittington;

To Caroline Cooper, for a highly professional proof read;

To Alfie Kohn, Malcolm Gladwell, Richard Koch, Fiona Harrold, Douglas Adams, Robert McKee and Charlotte Brontë, authors whose ideas have seeded and fed my own;

And to all the other people who have encouraged and helped me along the way;

Thank you.

All stories in this book are true from my current perspective, and part of my own history. Apologies to other participants in the events if they appear differently to your own memories of them.

For my brilliant mentor and role model
Lucy Whittington
and
sublime success coach
Dave Kibby

who each separately told me
I had to write this book.

STORIES FROM AN EFFORTLESSLY CREATED LIFE

Starting point

You know those IQ puzzles that were fashionable for a while as Christmas presents? They were usually made of wood, often with a twisty bit of wire and some rings you had to get off it, or some 3D shapes you had to put together into other 3D shapes.

I used to bash my head against these things. Till about the age of 15 I'd pick them up and try to force them into cooperation. I'd try them every way, getting more and more frustrated.

Then one day – when someone else was doing one, and I couldn't get my hands on it, only watch – I discovered that if I sat back and just looked at it, not particularly "trying" to solve it, just turning it in my mind without any particular thought, there would come a moment when I just knew.

From there I could walk over and with one or two effortless movements, the loop would be off the wire and it would be done. It is a delicious sensation, that moment of knowing: nothing physical seems to change, except perhaps there is a slight smile. It is the moment of creation, something coming from nothing. Knowledge appears where knowledge did not exist before.

Life is easy for me – at least the external bits. I must confess to a bit of unnecessary complication in the emotional things: relationships, personal development, managing my wild ambition – but for the practical things, the projects that tug at my heart, providing for the people around me, creating the environment I desire, making things happen, easily and quickly, I seem to have that mastered.

So someone suggested I write a book about it, describing how that happens for me, in case anyone else is interested in mastering it, too.

Consider the possibility that everything is much, much, much easier than it seems

I have this theory that everything is easy. It's just about our way of looking at things. If we've done something before, and it's worked, then we tend to do it the same way next time. In one sense this is efficient but it can mean we miss the opportunity to find a much, much, much easier way.

I used to run a home staging company, helping people set up houses for sale. It was my job to arrange a house so it appealed to people, so that potential buyers would walk in and feel good, be able to see themselves living there, and at least one or two of them would make an offer to buy.

It made the process of selling and buying houses easier for everybody, and that's a good thing, right? Making something that is often a big deal, easier – that's a good idea. I think so.

I'll tell more stories from that time later, but the one I'm thinking of now is how I generated business for that business, how I got the phone ringing, the calls coming in. That piece is critical for any business, and for a one person business, like mine was, it's critical to make it happen without it taking too much time.

I tried lots of different things to do that, lots of different things that challenged me, like picking up the phone, talking to people, speaking at real estate sales meetings, telling them about what I did.

I tried spending money on advertising (which didn't work at all); I tried dropping leaflets to houses where there were For Sale signs (which didn't work either).

Then one day I put several pieces of information together, and a simple solution crystallised, that moment of creation, something from nothing.

I had been aware for a while that the receptionists at real estate offices are often overlooked. People want to speak to the agent, and the person who connects you is just part of that mechanical process. I was never comfortable about this, so I made a point of making a personal connection with that person, even if just momentarily, as the call was being put through.

If I was doing a presentation or delivering training to the agents, I'd bring an extra information pack, including chocolates, and give it to the receptionists.

Then one day, an agent told me, "I never keep the fliers myself. If I want someone to do something, I just ask the girl at the desk who to call."

At that moment something clicked into place, and I went home and did up a letter especially for the receptionists, with a list of triggers:

> if you hear someone say this...
>
> if you notice that...
>
> if an agent says, "I hate doing open homes at that house, it's depressing"
>
> if a home owner says, "I don't know how I'm going to get the house ready in time"

and I said, "If you hear someone say one of these things, give them my card."

I bought some flier stands, put the letters into envelopes with more chocolates, and dropped into a real estate office I was passing. I chatted to the receptionist, whom I'd met and chatted to briefly before; I asked her name, and the name of the others who worked on reception, and I wrote those names, one on each envelope, and left those and the stand full of fliers behind.

I did that six times, to six different offices, over the next six weeks and after that I never had to market that business again.

Five minutes a week, for six weeks, and it was done forever.

I have a theory that for every business, there is a similarly effortless way of marketing. Either it takes that little time, or it's something you enjoy doing so much – like going to the pub and telling stories, or going out to coffee with friends – that you'd do it anyway, whether or not it was bringing you business.

If you're not in business, or you work in a bigger organisation where you don't have to do the marketing and sales, this story may not have as much meaning for you. That's okay, I've got loads more. The point is, for everything, there is ALWAYS an easier way.

What if the project you thought would be your life's work could be done in ten months, and easily delegated? What would you do then?

Reticular activating system

Some people abbreviate this to RAS. That's just annoying, in my view. How would you ever remember what that stands for?

Your reticular activating system is the function of your brain that filters the information coming in through your senses and highlights things that are relevant to you. It's why in a room full of different conversations, at a party, perhaps, you immediately hear if someone says your name. It's why you are so aware of cars the same as yours. It's why the public toilet signs in airports are so much more visible at some times than others.

The reticular activating system is essential for our sanity in this fast-paced world. I experienced the reverse of it for a while after having surgery to correct partial hearing loss. The two weeks afterwards nearly drove me mad while my brain adjusted to filtering the sounds that were coming in that ear. Picking up my children from school was overwhelming, until that brain filter adjusted, and once again my attention was only drawn to things that were relevant to me.

I tried some experiments with my reticular activating system, very simple experiments, shifting my awareness of colour. I was driving back from seeing some friends in the country, and I asked my reticular activating system to look for the colour red. For a few seconds nothing happened, and then my eyes were drawn to a sign partially hidden and shaded by some trees. There was a small patch of red on it.

Next I tried yellow, and almost instantly, the double lines marking a stop sign on a side road (it was New Zealand, where those lines are yellow) shot into my field of vision like arrows. By this point, two minutes into the experiment, I was realising there was something in this.

Next I tried blue. Immediately I spotted a faded piece of farm machinery, an auger, in a nearby field. A moment of quiet followed, and then, in a telescoping shift of perspective, the whole sky came into focus, seeming to enlarge and come at me, pushing me back in my seat, eyes wide.

This was powerful, but another more powerful example came a few weeks later, as we were heading to my parents-in-law's beach house, a six-hour drive from home. We were driving through a town in a mountain pass, and I tried the experiment again, with similar, although by now less surprising results. We had come out the other side of the town when I selected purple as my next colour to highlight. For the next ten minutes I remained lightly aware of it, but there just was no purple. Conversation took over, and other wide-ranging thoughts, and I forgot about it.

We stopped in at the family farm, had a cup of tea, caught up with news, picked up the key and drove out to the beach. We were chatting as we carried in the luggage, walked in through the kitchen, and then as I got a few steps into the house I was hit as if by a physical force with two small patches of colour on the notice board – two photographs amongst the sea of pictures pinned to the board, one of my sister-in-law, one of my niece, each happening to be wearing a purple dress.

I had forgotten, but the unconscious process of my reticular activating system was still working away at the instruction I had given it over three hours before.

That was when I recognised its power.

Open your mind to seeing the impossible

All it takes to see the impossible is a "what if" attitude, the suspension of disbelief. Just be lightly interested in the possibility of finding what you want, no matter how unlikely. Ask your reticular activating system to look out for something new, an easy solution, and forget it. There's nothing to lose... unless you have some ulterior motive, some hidden reason for not wanting to achieve the things you say you do.

In my experience, this hidden ulterior motive issue is much more common than it appears, in this world where we do things the same way, for the same predictable result. In my work it's common for clients to freak out when we bring their stated goal rapidly closer. There's often a moment of panic before a new obstacle appears to make them feel safe again.

For some it's just the speed; for others, actually it's the achievement of the goal itself that scares them. In my world where anything is possible, and everything is easy, these demons come up again and again.

Which presents me with an interesting challenge: how do I recognise and select clients who can cope with this pace of change and success? Or is there a way I can train them, make them feel safe through the process so they can adjust?

My good friend Martha Grover of JDV London explained this to me. She works with people to make big changes in health and lifestyle, body, nutrition, style, home and managing roles in life. About six months ago, as we were making radical changes to my body, my shape, the way I move, with almost no sense of effort on my part, she explained the brain science to me.

If we feel safe, change is effortless, easy. If we push ourselves, force ourselves to exercise or eat a certain way, the brain senses danger and works hard to preserve the status quo.

The classic line through this process came from me: "Martha, what happened? My calves are a different shape, there are muscles, and we didn't do any exercise." She just smiled.

So my current challenge is to do the same for my clients: create a match of speed and possibility and expectation, and a safe space for that huge change to happen.

It's a work in progress. I'll keep you posted.

EASY

STORIES FROM AN EFFORTLESSLY CREATED LIFE

A project-based life

The work I do is project-based: decide on something worthwhile to do, see a clear, defined end point, usually within a very short time frame, and go at it till it's done. I love working this way. Just writing that sentence I can feel energy accelerate as it moves through my heart and chest.

At the moment, many of my projects are books, working with speakers and other experts whose ideas flow better in speaking than in writing; they might be in their best flow on stage, or in conversation. I capture their message in their words, by recording their speaking events, or by pre-agreeing a structure and doing a series of interviews, then I take that spoken content and shape it into a book.

The process is effortless for the speaker, requiring three to four relatively relaxed days of their time, and easy for me.

The main issue I deal with is helping them adjust to the ease and speed of it.

Most people, when they think of writing a book, work on something like a year as a time frame. Using my interview/recording process we can have a first draft to look at within a week.

The completion takes longer, around six weeks, because good editors usually have a waiting list and proofreaders have other things happening in their lives.

For the author, too, time to catch up with what's happening as they review each draft seems to be a good thing. They maintain that critical element of feeling safe, making the experience positive rather than terrifying – a good business aim for me, if I want any kind of repeat.

And I love repeat business, working with the same client again and again – it smoothes things out, reduces the need to explain my way of working, makes my projects faster, more efficient, and my life more productive.

I think that's maybe where all this came from... there is so much I want to get done in my life. By definition, if I finish each thing faster, I can fit more in.

I love Richard Koch's book, *The 80/20 Principle*. Do the 80% that you can do in 20% of the time, and wherever possible, let go of the last 20% that would chew up the remaining 80% of the time.

When I was staging houses, I came to have another view of this, another perspective: in any particular instance, with any particular person or family, there is a way to arrange things that is 100% perfect; when you are arranging to appeal to the widest cross-section of the market, conversely, the last 20% will be a matter of personal opinion – some people like this colour scheme, some like that.

There are some universal principles that apply to make people feel comfortable, to help them move through a home, to give them a sense of light and space. Beyond that, you can't please everyone, so it's okay, even logical, to stop at the 80%, not try to make it perfect. In that context there's no such thing.

Let me elaborate...

EASY

The three concepts of home staging that produce 95% of the result, and can be taught in ten minutes

Over seven years of working in this area, and a previous year of working for a real estate company, and with my irrepressible natural tendency to observe and refine and experiment, I came up with many, many ideas and instincts about what to do and how, to make the biggest impact on how a house looks and feels, in the shortest amount of time.

I also refined these ideas, these guiding principles, until I narrowed the list down to three that gave almost all the result with minimal effort.

They are:

1. Our eyes don't scan a whole space – we look from point to point to point in a predictable pattern, so that if we put the best pieces of art and furniture in the primary view lines, we can quickly maximise visual impact

2. Our sense of space is not governed by the size of the room, but by how far we can see. This means that if we can open a door or remove curtains to provide a view through, or hang a mirror to give a reflection, either to a visual focal point on the other side of the room, or, better still, to a view through a door or window, people's sense of space will be greatly increased

3. People can only take in a limited amount of visual information in a short space of time – we can make sure they see and remember what is important by simplifying and using visual themes

There are many more concepts – in fact even two years after moving out of this business I still surprise myself by coming out with well thought-out opinions on any aspect of home styling and arrangement, and how people need to see and feel before they buy – things I hadn't realised I'd thought about, and never heard myself express before.

Coming up with them is just a result of focus and attention; the ability to apply the knowledge more broadly grows naturally, through the process of doing something and thinking about it over time.

There are more concepts but just these three produce spectacular results. There were often audible gasps from audiences through my Before and After presentation, even more satisfying when I went back to the before picture, and then back to the after, and heard the gasp again.

Three guiding concepts, spectacular results. Easy.

EASY

Self-hypnosis

One of my clearest stories of being led by intuition centres around a pivotal day in my life: the day I learned self-hypnosis.

It was a strange sequence of events. I'd been playing with intuition, trying out what I could do with it, and one Saturday I tuned in to see what would be a good thing for me to do with the day. "Go out to Kaiapoi to Lizzie B's" was the message. Lizzie B's was a local cinema; it had a café and screening room with sofas and comfortable chairs. I'd never been to a film there, just dropped in to buy takeaway coffee when I was staging a house out that way, and thought it looked fun.

So I drove out, not too far, but out of town, and discovered it was closed. "Till further notice. Sorry for any inconvenience."

"So what am I doing here?" I wondered. The hit to go there had been so clear. I turned around in the car park, and felt an intuitive pull towards a health food shop on the other side of the group of businesses. I'm not really a health food shop person, but I followed the pull and walked over. And it was closed, too, for the weekend.

Again, odd.

I peered through the window, and there was a display board just inside the door. I am sure there were other things on the board, but I didn't see any of them, just a small flier about a self-hypnosis course which leaped out at me, vivid, in contrast to its actual format and printing. I read the web address, the course title, then turned again, wondering what I was going to do now.

In the end I got back in my car, had a pleasant drive in the country and went home, forgetting all about the earlier events of the day.

Then ten days later, the image of the flier jumped back into my mind, hit me head on, as if someone had held it up right in front of my eyes. I went to the Internet, typed in the web address and found it was the last day of the early bird special. The message was clear. Sign up.

I did that one-day course and learned the techniques which over the next few weeks I refined down from a 20-minute process to around 20-30 seconds. Then using that process, I introduced some of the most profound changes into my ongoing life. One of those I'll go into at more length later.

I still use self-hypnosis in an extremely efficient form, almost every day, to streamline and accelerate the things I do in life.

EASY

Easy books

As I mentioned, some of my current work is with speakers and other experts, writing their books.

I've been writing since I was six, worked on different projects, on and off. At around fifteen I was swayed by the advice of my parents and teachers, and took a long, dark detour into the world of science and IT. Thankfully I'm back now, and able to use all that experience in my new projects and life.

For my own books, which so far have been mostly novels about women in business, the process is streamlined. I write every day, because I love it and I'm horrible to live with if I don't. I promise myself to write for at least five minutes every day, which is enough time for me to reconnect with the story; most days, those five minutes turn into an hour.

My consistent writing rate is 1,500 words an hour: so, for a 60,000 word novel, the first draft is done in around 40 hours, over six or seven weeks. Usually when I get near the end, I'll do the last 10,000 words in a run, over two days. The story just seems to take hold at that point, ready to be finished in a coherent rush.

I find working in this way creates a single creative arc for the book, one creative movement – which means there's not much editing and almost no restructuring required. It's as if I can hold it all in my head for that long, linking backwards and forwards effortlessly, unconsciously. If I take a break of more than a day during the process, that single arc is broken, and it needs far more work to get to a finished product.

Once the draft is done, I leave it a few days, and then do a complete edit in a single run. I put aside two days for this, taking frequent short breaks, but once again, holding the whole work in my head for the time of editing. It's mostly line edits – refining word choice, bringing more elegance to a sentence here and there, and perhaps correcting things like an unintentional name change for a character or smoothing out the time sequence. Small things.

I like to refine the layout at this point in the process. There's something very relaxing about letting the words flow through my fingers and I check the chapter length, move chapter starts to a right-hand page, manage paragraph layout and justification, and the like, without having to make any judgement on the words themselves.

Writing is a flow; editing involves assessment and judgement to improve the overall quality of the work. For me, that takes resilience. Layout is different. Doing the layout is like brushing the hair of someone you love. You're presenting the story to the world with its face washed and its clothes ironed.

White space allows the reader space to reflect. A beautiful font is restful and pleasing to the eye. This is where the love shows, visually; it's easy and enjoyable and relaxing to do. Like a holiday amid the more strenuous activity of the production.

Now the manuscript gets printed out and sent off to a professional editor, to add the final polish, and highlight any remaining rough edges. My editor, Tanya, was a childhood friend. We used to write together when we were twelve. She edits full time now, and it's a complete gift for me to work with her at this stage of the projects that are so personally important to me.

I add in Tanya's edits, check the layout again, then print once more and send the final draft to proofreaders, to root out any remaining typos and practical errors.

Normally by now I've got the cover well underway. At some stage I will have been inspired to write a blurb and send a brief to my graphic designer, who produces three or four sketched ideas for me to choose from. In one instance, I took the first cover she sent; at the other end of the spectrum, for *Slow Time* we took ten or more attempts to get to the right place. My gut instinct is clear when I see the ideas: yes or no. If it's no, I usually put some thought into why not, so the next round is more likely to yield success.

The last phase is to integrate any corrections from the proofreaders and my own final read-through, create the PDF and upload the cover and content to the print-on-demand websites I use. I also run the text through the Smashwords.com style guide process, and upload to Smashwords for propagation of the book to all the major eBook sites. HUGE thanks to Mark Coker for this fantastic service to independent authors.

And then, the celebration! Another book done. The process as a whole takes two months for the writing and two months for the production – I have these staggered so that I am writing the next book while the previous one is being produced.

EASY

Books with clients

The process for writing books with clients is even faster, and even easier for the client, although for me there are a couple of additional steps.

Most of the people I work with already have a well-honed message – they know what they want to say, and have usually said it many, many times before. The trick is that most of them are better as speakers than they are as writers: they are more fluent and produce better, clearer ideas at the speed of speech than at the speed of writing.

I also add the advantage of being a fascinated listener. You know how when someone is very interested in what you are saying, you get more excited, speak more fluently, engage with your topic, explore it more fully? The more interested the audience, the better you communicate. So it's my job to be the professional audience. I'm fascinated by the ideas, skills and knowledge of others, which brings synergy to the process in which I interview and they speak.

First we work on an outline, and with my background in software design this is very natural for me.

Then we plan a couple of chapters in detail, and let it sit for a day or two. I suggest they think of stories to illustrate their points, because it is stories we learn from at a deep level. They're easy to listen to, we engage with them, and then generalise from there to our own lives. Filling a book with stories is a great way to create impact with the message we have to share.

Then we do the interviews, one or two chapters at a time. A book of 30-40,000 words requires about five to six hours of fluent interview, so that can be done fairly quickly. A couple of days is optimum for me – three hours a day of recording is relaxed and fun. To do it all in a day is possible, but doesn't leave time for the social chat and bounce of ideas that I love to intersperse into the process.

We get those interviews transcribed – or if the author has already delivered the exact content live and recorded it, we can work with that. I do a first pass at the edit, shifting the content from spoken grammar, which is more flexible and changeable than we expect to see on the page, into written format.

I love this part of the process: it's easy, and you get a real sense of the content, and the voice of the speaker. Retaining the speaker's voice is the first priority for me, so I polish that up just enough that it reads intelligently and well.

Then we get together and discuss the work so far. Is it shaping up as they expected? Are there any changes they would like made?

There is another edit, another check with the author, and then we are into the same production schedule of professional edit, proofreading and cover design that I use for my novels. Easy.

The author spends about four days, plus their proofread, and the book is done. Their message, their voice, a fun process in a tiny amount of their time.

EASY

Finding the boat

Sometimes all you need to do to get what you want is ask for it.

My novel *Moment of Change* is set in Picton, a harbour town at the top of the South Island of New Zealand, from which the inter-island ferry comes and goes. When I was writing that book, there were two pieces of essential research: first, I needed to find a pub where working people would go to drink – not the chi-chi tourist places that line the waterfront, but somewhere down-to-earth, probably with beer stains on the tables; and second, I needed to know something about boats. My protagonist was new to life on the water, but she got a job at a boat yard, and my grasp of the terminology was tenuous.

Now comes one of those stories I can't explain with logic. It was a simple thing, but clear, obvious and bizarrely improbable. I had in the back of the mind I needed to find the working man's pub, and, in an apparently unrelated incident, my intuition one morning was pushing me hard to call a particular friend and ask to meet for coffee. "No," was my immediate response, "I've got other things I need to do." Intuition was insistent, however, so I called his mobile.

"I'd love to, but I can't, I'm on the ferry, about an hour out of Picton."

"Going north or south?"

"South, coming home."

"Well then, while you're there, would you mind...?"

As easy as that. Philip is brilliant at any kind of random brief, and he found the pub – not where I expected, but several blocks back from the water, up the hill, on the road out of town. He photographed it inside and out so I could describe it, and sent me a Google map of its location so I could complete the picture. All done; and it kept the story on track: if I'd found it later, I'd have had to re-work a lot of things, to alter the location in retrospect.

For the boating lessons, it was a similar thing. I was at my coaching session (I've had the amazing Saskia Clements as my coach for life, business and anything else you can think of, for the past nine years) and I found myself saying "I need to find someone with a boat, someone who can tell me all the words for things."

"Well, we're going out on my dad's boat, the weekend after next, if you want to come and have a look. It's up in the Marlborough Sounds, though, in Picton. Are you okay driving that far?"

"Picton? Really? Perfect!"

I went up, took a deep breath and did another bit of research, walking into the backpackers next to the rail yard, and spending the night there, with trains being shunted back and forth till 4.30 a.m. The next morning I met Saskia and Tim. Tim spent an hour with me, showing me over the boat, telling me all the names for things, with me taking copious notes; then they took me out on the water, across the sound, for a glorious morning tea, talking about writing, books, business. I've never felt more looked after.

In the afternoon I took the car along Queen Charlotte Drive to Havelock – a road that later became a central location in the story. Then I drove home, everything done, and with a much better feel for the town, too: the atmosphere of the light towards sunset, the shape of the houses on the hills, and the roads connecting them.

There was another bonus: on the way I resolved a story issue that had been bothering me, and that gave the book a completely different direction and feel from that moment on. Applying deep breathing, extra oxygenation to my brain, and the colour and movement of the road beneath my wheels, the hills I was driving through, allowed inspiration to flow in an unexpected way.

"My foes are not of my own household"

Looking back, one of my most important lessons about how to live a full and satisfying life came from Charlotte Brontë's book *Shirley*. One of the characters is a young mill owner, Robert, working hard to repay the debts of his bankrupt family. His sister, Hortense, is obstinate and somewhat ridiculous, but he treats her with kindness; he also suggests having his eccentric mother-in-law move in, and when questioned by his fiancée about his willingness, gives this as part of his answer: "[My] foes never have been, nor ever will be, those of [my] own household."

This opened my eyes to the conflict I had often seen around me, where people compete, fight or argue with the people they live with. I loved the idea of living differently, of supporting and nurturing those closest to me.

And that is how I have lived since then: offering that support, encouraging the dreams of my husband and my children. It makes life so much simpler, is so much more pleasant, conserves so much energy, which is then available for me to use to live my dreams.

There is a related phenomenon, possibly the cause of the other. I have observed it frequently with my two cats, and less frequently with my two children – it is that situation where a person or animal has an excess of energy, is in the mood to start a fight. With the cats, and with young children, the spat flares up, creates a temporary scene and noise, then dies down, forgotten.

I think what sometimes happens with adults is that we take this for more than it is – for more than a temporary expression of a temporary emotion. We build a problem around it, and go looking for it to rear up again, or go looking for solutions.

I know about myself that very simple things can affect my mood. I think something big and important is going wrong, then someone brings me a sandwich, I eat it, and suddenly all is right with the world.

Keep close, continue loving and supporting the people around you, and watch the effortlessness of life unfold.

Easy decisions

Sometimes the hardest thing is not the doing; it is the deciding to do. So it makes sense to make that easy, too.

Intuition plays a big part here, as well. You can't decide these things by logic – there's too much to consider, too much you can't know until you get started.

One of the things experience has taught me over the years is that knowing what not to do is as important as choosing which opportunities to take.

Looking back, there are several points in my life where I appear to have gone off track: my career in computer science, or buying thirteen house lots of furniture for my business when one of my fundamental priorities in life is travelling light…

I don't like to think of these things as mistakes; rather they have been opportunities to learn, through the experiences they provided, and through the contrast with the aspects of life that buzz me more.

Lately my hit rate has improved, I'm more clearly on my path, but I still use and benefit from everything I have learned along the way.

Two obvious points of highly tuned clarity were the time I decided to go to New York to do Robert McKee's *Story* course, and the time I decided to publish my first book.

The first decision I had been struggling with for a little while. I had read McKee's book and was strongly drawn to attend the course in New York, for some reason – although the alternative option of Australia would have been far more practical from where I lived at the time, in New Zealand. The cost of the course was modest, but the costs of the airfares and the hotel were not.

So I went to see Saskia, my coach, who took me through an intuitive exercise. "Imagine yourself on a forest path, and you come to a place where the path splits. In one direction is you going to New York; in the other direction is you not going. Follow each one along a little way, and tell me what you see."

It was so clear, I almost laughed. On the path of going to New York, attending the course, was a summer garden, full of flowers and colour and light. On the other path the branches were withered and dead, and the path ended just a few metres along from the split.

"I guess I'm going."

"I guess you are."

The second decision, to publish my first book, had been brewing for much longer, but not getting any clearer. Then one day in December 2009 I tuned into my intuition, asking what was the next step in furthering my success as a writer.

The answer baffled and annoyed me: "Go to the networking event at the bierkeller tonight."

"What???"

I couldn't think of anything worse: loud music, and people whom I liked on a Thursday morning over an orderly breakfast now in an environment where drinking was the purpose of the night.

"Really? Really? (sigh) Oh, okay."

It was so clear, there was no arguing, but it was so illogical, so not what I wanted to do, that I argued anyway. I went, grumbling all the way.

Even after that night I couldn't see the point. I had met some nice people, had a few nice chats, and left before anyone became untidy. Perhaps when I got home I wondered, "What was all that about?" – perhaps not. Perhaps I just forgot about it, until five months later, when I met one of those nice people again.

My friendship with Liz blossomed rapidly. We found we had a lot in common. She was starting a new business, and since I fitted her ideal client profile I offered my perspective about what would attract me to use her service.

At the end of that meeting she asked if she could read one of my books. I emailed them all to her; she picked one and read it in one sitting, on a Saturday morning, four hours curled up on the sofa in her pyjamas.

We met again, and somehow during that meeting it became clear I was going to publish. I'd had lots of discussions with publishing companies, got near to publication more than once. It was time to do it myself.

The way I remember it, it wasn't even a decision, or rather the moment of decision was so smooth, so easy, it didn't feel momentous, just natural.

We planned the book launch for four months later – she offered her beautiful central-city foot clinic as the venue. "Does that give you enough time?"

"Yes, heaps."

"Do we need to make a list of what you need to do to get the book published in that time?"

I thought about this for a moment. "No, I think it's all pretty clear."

In fact the book was printed and ready to sell ten weeks after that conversation. Towards the end of that ten weeks I'd had a week in England, in Cornwall with my lovely friend Diane, to mark the change from not published to published, for me a watershed in my life... It hadn't been a time of mad activity at all: it had been ten weeks of lightly holding the vision of it, and finding others to do the work for me.

The launch itself was even easier. I love the way Liz and I work together. The space she had created for her business was beautiful – clean space, red sofas, colour, texture, and visual focus on red roses in single-stem vases evenly spaced on cut-outs in smooth white walls.

I sent out invitations and people were so kind, so excited about me following this dream that we had 80 people respond, "Yes". Liz bought cheese and wine and olives and crackers, hired glasses and plates; I picked up the baguettes from our local French bakery, and it was done.

On the evening there was a buzz, I was alive with joy, Liz made it all easy. My friend Stuart took payment for the books so I had time to sign them and talk; I gave an impromptu speech, not planned or even thought about in advance, thanking the people who had been part of the process: Jay who designed the cover; Lynley from the printing company; my family; Liz.

My writing buddy, Kerrin, was there, the one who gave me my first deep recognition as a writer.

It was a glorious night. Such a huge moment in my life, and so effortlessly achieved. Thank you, Liz! And thank you to Joanne, who arranged the networking event at the bierkeller – who would have thought?

EASY

Sometimes we confuse important with difficult

Try this statement on for size:

> *The more important something is, the harder it will be to do...*

Does it sound logical, plausible? But then, why should that be? Why should it take a lifetime of dedicated work to change something significant? What if that could be easy and fast, too?

This morning I have come up with a model for the easy project process. I've been a little frustrated recently, actually because I don't have enough to do.

When everything is easy, this can become the challenge. You find something to do, you do it, it's done, and you're looking around for the next thing.

Or it's not done, but it's in one of those phases where it is waiting on something else to happen. You've done what you need to do; the next step is up to someone else, or it's just not the right time yet.

This is why it's so important to collaborate with other people who know everything is easy, and that things can be done fast. Otherwise you drive yourself crazy waiting for others to take necessary action.

The first phase, then, is finding a project. Sometimes I overlook this: I beat myself up for getting nothing done, when in fact there is nothing to do. When things happen rapidly, easily, you are always looking for something new to do.

If you're interested, here is my guide to the creative project process – adapt it to suit, or ignore it completely and go with your gut.

Jennifer's creative project guide

Phase one: find a project that engages and excites you, that is worth doing, where you can see the goal, and that goal will hold your attention to the end.

Phase two: define the project. On your own, or it's more fun with others, define the constraints that will fire your creativity. Robert McKee talks about the power that constraints give to our creative capacity. A completely open field leaves us bored; working within constraints engages us.

What result do we want, in clear, specific terms? Who do we want to work with? How do we want to feel? What would enable us to enjoy it more? What would give the outcome even more impact, more value? Do we want to work within certain hours, or in a certain location? Are there financial constraints of input, or specific financial goals of output?

Ask as many questions as you like, come up with as many specifics as you feel pulled to. The unconscious mind has infinite capacity to find solutions, infinite capacity to work with whatever conditions we give it; the reticular activating system has awesome power to find whatever we ask it to find. Have fun. Use these things to make what you are doing exponentially more powerful.

Phase three: contemplate. Think about the project. Write things down. Stare out the window. Go for a drive. Get on a train or a boat or a plane and allow your thoughts to swirl and move and settle, allow yourself to forget about the project in the lightest, easiest way.

Allow easy to appear. Allow the genius solution to float or explode into your mind. Allow the laughter of recognition, the joy of spontaneous creation. It is at these moments I feel closest to being the expression of God, the expansion of the New Universe.

Phase four: action the easy. Once you have the easy solution in mind, put it into action. Take the small, easy steps; pull in the people who appear, ready to do the other pieces; find the people who will be inspiring to collaborate with, and inspire and ignite them with your Why, your vision of what this project could and will be.

Phase five: complete. Bring action to the defined conclusion. Actually finish it. See the vision, hold the vision, bring the vision into reality. Take the final actions that bring it to a close, ready for the next project to appear in the vacuum.

Phase six: celebrate. This is essential, the acknowledgement to those awesomely powerful forces – the unconscious mind and the reticular activating system – that their efforts have been worthwhile. This is the joy of life, the equivalent of God's seventh day (it may seem presumptuous, that we're getting ahead of God, but the phases often take longer than a day so we aren't, really). Sit back and survey your creation. Enjoy it, revel in it.

Phase six is also the time for looking back and integrating learning. What has this journey taught you? What have you received as side effects from achieving the clear goal? Do you have new friends, new people to draw on? Have you learned new skills? Have you had the opportunity to visit new places? Have new opportunities arisen out of this path, this project?

Phase seven: enjoy the afterglow. Take a break. This is magic time, dreaming time, empty, nothing, everything-is-possible time. Allow it to sit, empty, and just be. Out of this time, at the right time, something new will emerge. Trust that, and allow yourself to glory in this space.

EASY

Abundance of oxygen

One of the things that sometimes trips us up is the sense that resources are finite: "If I only had enough money"; "if I only had enough time"; "if I only had more confidence, more wit, more friends or more good ideas".

What if all resources were infinite – or, at least, so abundant that we could never run them dry?

Even if you're sceptical, try the thought experiment. How would life change if you had all the money you could need for what you want to do? Sometimes it's a bit of a shock to realise how little would alter, minute to minute.

I once did an exercise, to write down ten things billionaires do that don't cost any money. It was easy. Do it yourself now, if you like. I'll start you off:

1. Sit around drinking coffee, talking to good friends
2. Walk on the beach
3. Play with their children, or their grandchildren, or their friends' children
4. Read an inspiring book
5. Stare out the window dreaming of what they will do with their lives

See, it's easy.

And I remember the slight shock when I realised that even if I were as wealthy as I could wish or imagine, I would still be twelve kilograms overweight (that's sorted now, and it was easy… more about that later).

There's a story in Dale Carnegie's book *How to Win Friends and Influence People*, about a very wealthy woman who took great pride in the diamonds she wore. Carnegie's comment was something like this: "If she had only taken the sour expression off her face and worn a smile, that would have made far more difference than the diamonds did."

There are always very simple things we can do in the moment that make more difference than the long-term, big-effort changes we might think we "should" make. Paying attention to posture, which we can change in a second, does more for how we look than losing a few kilograms, which will usually takes weeks or longer.

Spending half an hour clearing papers, straightening furniture, removing excess items, adding some fresh flowers, hanging a mirror or rearranging family photographs on a table can make more difference to the sense of space and energy of a room than a four-month, costly renovation.

If we're feeling rushed, taking thirty seconds, sitting in a comfortable chair from which we can see the sky through the window and allowing our thoughts to wander – or counting blessings, or thinking about an upcoming holiday, or the laughter of a good friend – can help us realise that we have plenty of time, we just fill it, without spaces. It's trying to do two, or three, or four things at once, or thinking about the next thing while we're doing this one, that makes us feel like time is in short supply.

What if we thought of all of these things in the same way as we think about air? For most of us, we just trust the supply of air. We breathe out trusting that there will be enough air to breathe in again. We don't even think about it – about the miracle that is – most of the time.

I'm not saying spend money you don't have, or put any more things into your day; I'm saying dream as if resources were limitless, and see where your imagination takes you.

And then possibly be brave enough to start living, in small or big ways, as if that were true.

You get what you ask for

When I started with Saskia as my coach I had modest aspirations. I had just started the idea of a business, and had no clients.

"I just want six clients," I said.

"And is that a stretch for you?" she asked, gently.

"I cannot imagine that it will ever happen. It seems impossible from here. Yes, it's a stretch."

"And will you be happy with that?"

"Ecstatic."

It was in the final week of the six-month coaching series that I got my sixth client. Saskia had gently suggested in the session before that I look at the possibility I might not reach my goal, and that we think about how I would handle that.

"I said six, and I'll get six," I declared. And I did.

"Right, now," I began, at the first session of the next series, "let's try for something bigger. I got exactly what I asked for last time, I assume I will this time, so let's make it worthwhile."

"Okay, what do you want?"

"By the end of the six months I want to have got to the equivalent of $100,000 turnover per year."

In that six months I turned over $50,040.

See? It worked.

I love applying this idea for others, too. One of my joys over the years has been bringing into reality the sometimes challenging requests in my children's letters to Father Christmas. It delighted me, their absolute confidence that what they asked for, whatever it was, would appear.

When I hear friends speak of their passions, their dreams, I highlight them, I point out the importance of what they have said, and I remind them if they later forget or deny it.

Sometimes there's something practical I can do to help it into existence; sometimes just holding the space for the possibility, telling them that of course it is possible, can be all someone needs.

I love having happy people around me. The most precious thing for me is when someone knows what they want and is happy when they get it.

If someone asks me for something, I'll go to the ends of the Earth to get it, apply everything I know to create it.

Sometimes I fail, which saddens me; but far more often I succeed.

EASY

I'm slower when I rush

We creative types don't really like deadlines. In some situations there's a panic-and-freeze response.

I completely believed this until a couple of weeks ago, when I was describing the phenomenon to my husband, Paul, on a lunch time walk.

"I'm a creator. I don't do things to deadline."

He nodded indulgently, as he has learned to do in the face of this kind of assertion. He knows there's more to come, and interrupting the flow at this point will slow down my thought process, and possibly result in unpleasant behaviour.

"Except when I'm writing articles. I can do that on a time frame. I wrote to deadline every month for six years."

Still he waits, listening.

"And my novels. I had deadlines for those, even though I set them myself."

Another nod.

"And when I was setting up houses. At the start I would panic and rush if I felt I didn't have enough time, but by the end I was able to move into that Slow Time feeling, where everything was effortless."

Still listening.

"So maybe I *can* do things to deadline. Maybe I can train myself to do other things this way, too."

After six years of furnishing houses, spending ten minutes in them then coming back days or weeks later with a truckload of furniture and accessories, I got into a pretty good rhythm. I started trusting my intuition for what to bring accessory-wise, rather than trying to work it out room by room in detail.

At the start I used to help the guys carry the light stuff into the house, to save them time, and me money, and because it didn't feel right to be standing around doing nothing while they worked.

This brings us back to phase three of the creative project process, the one that looks like sitting around doing nothing, and is actually the most powerful phase, where the unconscious takes over and works with possibilities, resources and details we could not possibly consciously contain.

After six years, I began to take a new approach. As soon as the guys had brought in the living room furniture, I would sit down, take a slow breath and relax. I had probably done a walk-through of the house by this point, brought in the bedding and cushions, which I usually carried in my car – probably I had, I don't remember. I just remember sitting in the space, doing "nothing", not a conscious thought in my head.

In this space, something magical happened. When the unloading was done, and the guys had gone, I began to move in slow motion. My body knew where each thing was going. The furniture was in place, and I might have directed some of the pictures to particular rooms; now just the hanging of the pictures, the making of the beds, the placing of accessories remained.

Previously, if I'd been in a hurry, I would find myself with narrow vision just handling one item at a time. In this different, flowing state, I would feel my hands pick up other items as I walked from one room to another, unconsciously bringing those items to where they needed to be.

Early on I'd developed a phrase that had helped me when I felt I didn't know what to do, when I was looking at too much at once: "Do the next obvious thing" – just like with writing a non-fiction book, there is always something obvious to do next.

It might be putting up a picture hook and hanging a picture. It might be making a bed, ironing the duvet in place, placing the cushions, smoothing extra blankets at the end for added colour. It might be clearing away packaging, taking it out to the car. It might be placing a vase on a kitchen bench, or on a dining table, or a coffee table.

There was always something obvious to be done.

And when there was nothing obvious left to do, I knew I was finished, job complete, time to go home and process the client's credit card payment. That was a good moment.

Staying in that slow-motion state of flow, that wide vision that allows you to move three objects at once, rather than making three single-focus trips, is a brilliant art to master. It might seem that it comes unbidden, that we don't control it, but in my experience that's not the case; we can create it at will.

It also might seem to be a mental state, but I don't think that's the case, either. It is closely linked to a physiological state, and by focusing on that, it is easy to change.

The first thing is breathing. We can slow our breath down and move it from chest (fight or flight mode) to belly (relaxed, confident mode). Then move our eyes around the edges of our visual field – if we're rushing, pushing things, our vision has probably become narrow – widening it out changes our mental state, too, slows us down so our actions are wider ranging, more creative, more effective.

In this state we can pull in resources we might have forgotten about in the narrow, fight or flight state; we come up with creative solutions. People love being around people who are in this state; it gives them confidence.

There are health benefits, too: digestion and the immune system function better, cell renewal happens, all sorts of really great things.

We often get to this point with things that we are practised at, and then something can tip us off balance, cause our state to change. Just a little attention can bring us back to our best.

There was a bit of frustration when I realised I was slower when I rushed things, and that I also produced an inferior result. So I worked out how to move Slow, even when I was short of time. Magic.

The art of delegation

Part of Easy projects is getting other people to do bits of them. This is easy, too, given that each step is easy, and there is always someone out there who loves doing it, who would be delighted to be asked, possibly to be paid, and especially to be part of your wider inspiring vision. If what we are doing engages and delights us, it's easy to have it engage and delight others, also.

My approach to delegation evolved naturally, I'm not sure when and how, but it's amazingly effective. It is to get one person to be in charge of each small, specific task. It's rare that I'll delegate two things to the same person.

I don't know if I had a reason for this at the start, but one result of it is that it's very easy to define that person's job, identify when it is done, thank them and show appreciation, and then move on to the next piece.

It also means that it is really obvious if they don't do what they are supposed to do, and then it's easy to have a conversation about it. "You said you'd deliver the furniture. Where is it?" "I was expecting the design by today. Is it ready?" Or more usually, "We said Tuesday for the design. Is that still okay for you?" which gives them time to make it okay, if it wasn't already on the way.

The key thing is to take any emotion out of the conversation, which allows for finding a solution. Like when my son had said he would mow the lawn, and then got busy having fun with his friends. "We said you'd mow the lawn today. When are you going to do it?" No anger, annoyance, upset; just a practical question.

Usually there would be an apology, but I really wasn't interested in that. It was the next bit that was interesting.

"I'll do it tomorrow after school."

"Great, thank you, that would be cool."

An interesting thing about this approach was that I had sometimes pre-paid him for the effort (if he was going to be paid, which he wasn't always, sometimes it was just part of family life) but he soon got to the point of only accepting money once he had done the job. He'd rather wait and have his moral freedom. This principle has carried through into choosing not to take out a student loan, but to manage the money as he goes.

For the production of my first six books, there was a team of eight people for each one. I wrote them, did some of the editing, and oversaw the project. I had Tanya to do the line edit, and sometimes to give me a pep talk if I thought the whole thing was terrible.

I had my cover designer, two other proofreaders and my printing account manager, Lynley, to oversee that side of things. Behind Lynley I know there was another whole group of people working, but from my perspective, she was the one who produced the magic goods.

Liz did the book launch, and there was the guy who provided and serviced my credit card machine, turning me into a one-woman mobile retail outlet. Brilliant.

There was also the lovely guy from my network group who sold me the special book-signing pens, but here we're getting a little beyond the immediate and essential scope of the project.

For staging houses, I had the moving guys, the courier company to pick up and return keys, and various suppliers, including Eco Frame and Mirror who several times provided picture hooks on an emergency basis when I ran out (the courier picked up and delivered these, too).

It's always easy to delegate a small, well-defined task, so I suppose part of making projects easy is being able to break them down into those small, well-defined pieces. Once you get used to it, that's also easy.

If a task doesn't look easy, see if there is some unnecessary emotion tied up around it. That conversation about my son not mowing the lawn could have been emotional, a conflict. It wasn't. It's always possible to take the emotion out and deal with the facts. "You said you'd deliver the furniture. Where is it?"

Learning to shut up and listen

The professional interview part of my business grew out of a frustration I have sometimes had about myself: that when I meet someone interesting I get so excited about their ideas that I take up those ideas and run with them, and don't listen enough to what the person has to say.

I came home after an evening at the National Speakers' Association one evening, hugely frustrated with myself. "I met so many fascinating people, why didn't I shut up and listen to them?"

I went to bed pondering this idea, and woke up with a solution. If I started a business as a professional interviewer, people would pay me to shut up and listen. I would get to sit and listen and learn, drinking in everything they had to say, and I'd actually get paid for it. Brilliant!

Even more brilliant, my clients loved it. People hardly ever get to experience a fascinated, engaged audience who says just enough to keep them talking, just enough to pull out their ideas and knowledge, and then goes quiet and lets them speak.

As a professional audience in a room full of professional speakers, I was like a boy at a dance class – an irony especially because this is a group of people who individually are most often the centre of attention because of their powerful, charismatic personalities.

A simple idea in response to an apparent problem. Genius!

In case you're interested, here is my simple strategy for world peace...

You know that little voice inside you that tells you what is right for you to do and what isn't? I don't mean "right" in a moral sense, something you could argue about or discuss; I mean it in the sense that it feels right, you just know it.

You know that voice?

It's my theory that that voice always leads us perfectly; and more than that, it fits us in with everyone around us, so that when others are following their voice, and we are following ours, the world fits together like a jigsaw puzzle and everything falls into place.

We don't need to think about what other people are doing – we only need to pay attention to ourselves, and what we are doing.

Even less than that, we don't need to do anything right away at all. We just need to listen to that voice, and if the thing we are about to do does not feel right, we just don't do it. Do nothing.

Within minutes, another action, another option will appear. Check that as well – if your internal voice and feeling tell you it's right, do it; if not, don't, and wait for the next idea to come along.

Let's look for a moment at all the things around us that seem to cause problems – pulling triggers, making guns, mindless consumption of resources. If we just stopped taking those actions, almost all of our current "problems" would disappear.

As for what happens next, once we start taking the right actions, the gut actions, the things we know in our hearts are what we are supposed to do... Imagine that. Imagine what would happen then.

Writing in France

I often have the experience of writing something in my journal and having events magically follow. It was in November of 2010 that I wrote, "I'd like to be fluent in French."

Two days later Paul phoned from work and said, "You know how we were planning to travel again in a couple of years, once the children have left school? How would you feel if that were sooner? Because I may have the opportunity of a transfer to France."

"That could work," I replied, thinking busily.

We had promised our children when we moved back to New Zealand seven years before that we wouldn't move again before they were ready to leave home. A lot had changed since then, however.

I knew our daughter would be delighted; it only remained to broach the subject with our son, who was then sixteen.

"How would you feel if we moved to France?"

"That's fine," he said, "but I'm not going."

"If you want us to stay here, we will."

"No, you need to do what's right for you," he responded, "but my life's here."

It was a tough call, leaving him behind, but not really. He was right: it was right for him and right for us and he was ready.

The move itself would have seemed major, except that everyone around us was dealing with bigger uncertainty.

Christchurch was in the first few months of the time of major earthquakes. None of us knew if our houses would be standing the next day. There was uncertainty whether we would live or die.

My not knowing whether or when I was moving to France, from one charmed life into another, did not raise much interest at all. I didn't even speak of it really, although of course I felt it.

It was five months before the transfer was confirmed; in the meantime we had sold our house knowing that, if we didn't go, it would not be easy to buy another home in the post-earthquake city. My gut just said the time was right.

Paul moved ahead of us, before the acquisition of the company he would work in was complete. I scheduled the movers before the confirmation came, and set the date for the flights, although they weren't booked for a while longer.

Paul set up our life in France; I closed down our life in New Zealand. We said goodbye, temporarily, to our son, and here we are, living a long-time dream, with no fuss, no drama – easy.

The only slightly surprising thing is that my French still has some way to go towards fluency. Curious. I wonder how that will turn out...

EASY

It's time to talk some more about intuition

For me, intuition is something I feel for and live by pretty much 100% of the time. I call on it for everything, from what to eat to when to make a phone call to which clients to choose, which projects to take on, what to say in any moment, any situation.

I felt the shift happen, from acting from apparent logic to this new way, a couple of years ago.

People refer to it by different names: inner guidance; innate wisdom; intuition; the voice of God. In the World Peace chapter I called it our inner voice.

Most of us have some understanding of it, some acknowledgement that, in the big things at least, we know deep down what is right for us.

I take it a step further, flowing my life from this source, with a sense of destiny about it. Even in the small things I listen for it, trust it, follow it; in fact, this is how I trained myself to listen for it, in the tiniest of things: I asked myself what I wanted to eat for breakfast.

Big decisions often come with a lot attached to them: preconceptions, fear of the unknown, concern for others. Fiona Harrold, in her book *Be Your Own Life Coach,* points out that it makes no difference to others what we eat for breakfast, and that we could have champagne and peaches if we chose.

So I started from here, a tiny moment, one early morning, when I was at the pantry deciding what to have. My normal breakfast was muesli with chocolate chips, but what did I feel like today? I listened, deep, to what came back from inside.

"Hot buttered toast with raspberry jam."

Simple enough, but we didn't have any raspberry jam in the house. We had strawberry jam, and we had the normal muesli, but to have raspberry jam I would have to get dressed and drive to the supermarket. Would it really make that much difference?

The answer is, yes. That moment when I chose to honour what I heard from deep in myself changed my whole life. I got dressed, drove to the supermarket, bought the jam, came home and ate breakfast.

From that moment on, the voice of intuition was familiar and clear in the big things also, because I had trained myself to recognise it in the tiny things.

And then, it is in the seemingly insignificant things that the biggest changes often come – things like which blog link to follow, which TED video to watch, whether to turn left or right, or go to the bierkeller or the movie theatre.

Sometimes this causes confusion around me, and I have to say, "I know! I know it doesn't look logical! I know it looks like I'm making a mess of things, like these events are upsetting me. I can't explain it but I know, I just know, this is right."

It can take courage to follow intuition, especially when the people who love us doubt it, but in another way it's easy, because there's not all that thought to process, the chasing of infinite cycles of logic, the endless weighing of options.

With intuition there is only one action, only one truth, in any moment.

That's not to say my actions don't usually look logical from the outside. Many of the things I do follow received wisdom. I attend appointments once they've been set; I make sales calls; I pay my bills and send out invoices.

It's more about timing, about the specific what and when; it's about knowing what not to do, about taking my time, focusing on what I'm doing now, trusting the future to the future. Living like the lilies of the field.

It's about allowing the magic of life to unfold, expressing the fullest version of me in the moment and trusting that the wisdom of my heart speaks the truth, in every moment.

And most of the time, it makes life easy.

More stories from a world of plenty

My husband Paul said "If you contrive to have plenty, then everything becomes simple." The question is, do you want it to be simple or not?

The other proviso I would put on this idea is that you have to feel like you have plenty – as with the oxygen we breathe, we have to feel the plenty so deeply we almost forget the resource is there at all. If we start worrying about oxygen, even if there is plenty, then life becomes very focused around that.

When my children were small, we had season passes to Legoland. It was around a 40-minute drive from where we lived, and we could go there whenever we liked, whenever the weather was pleasant, so we could stroll slowly, at our leisure, at the pace of the youngest child, weaving in and out of the families who had bought one-day tickets and were rushing from ride to ride, attraction to attraction, to make the most of their brief opportunity to experience.

If the crowds were thick, or the air turned cold, we might simply go home again, knowing we would come back another day.

We loved the puppet shows, so some days we would just do that: turn up on time for a showing, sit in each other's company and laugh at the slapstick jokes, most of which we had heard many times before.

There were rides we liked, some of which were easy to get on, others had longer queues. We could adapt on the day, decide whether to wait or not, depending on the length of the queue, our mood, how much we wanted that ride just then.

We could always come back, so our decision-making criteria were different from those of people who were only there for one day.

For the same reason, I always keep a fridge full of champagne. Somehow we've ended up with three fridges, and the largest one I bought with wine racks instead of shelves. It is always referred to as the champagne fridge, even though we store still whites there as well.

I don't drink much, and it's a while since a bottle was opened. It's nice on a Friday evening to fire a cork from the balcony and sit watching the sunset; but somehow, knowing it is there, that we could drink it any time, breakfast or lunch or dinner, means I think about it less. A world of plenty.

Often when I'm talking to people, the conversation circles around the resources that they don't think are plentiful. Sometimes that's money, sometimes that's time. I get a little frustrated, because there are so many other things I'd like to talk about.

There are so many ways we can make things happen other than by increasing our supply of the scarcest resource. One resource can often substitute for another – time for money, money for time (in the sense of delegation) at the simplest level.

For me it's so much more interesting to say what we want, without limits, and then allow it to unfold in surprising ways. It makes a better story if you can create something without money, anyway, if it comes to you by a series of coincidental events, in a surprising way.

I like plenty of the simple pleasures: bath salts, fresh towels, crisp linen for the bed. Other types of plenty – possessions, excess body from excess consumption of food – come with challenges of their own.

It's just about how we look at what we've got. I have plenty of everything I need. I know this, because everything it occurs to me to desire comes to me, usually very quickly, and with a great story attached.

Do you really want it?

My experience is, if people are making something hard work, it's either because they think everything is hard work, or because they are not totally sure they want the result they are heading for.

The thing you are working on, do you believe it is possible? Have you thought about the way you want it to happen? Are you okay with the ways life will change once you've got it?

I get so clear about the reality of the things I see in the future – my life adapts to incorporate them before they are physically real.

If something about what you want to achieve makes you unsure, or worry about losing something you have – it may be a friend, a relationship, even free time – it can appear that the details of moving towards it, the steps required, are difficult, and most often you will let go of it, not make it happen.

There's something else that comes up for people, too, something that is apparent by its absence, if that makes sense – in the things they don't say. Once again, it's an underlying assumption that is invisible because it is accepted as deep reality for those who hold it. I call it "the last biscuit on the plate fallacy".

Remember the days of visits from relatives, when the good biscuits were put out, and our eyes were out on covetous stalks, the desire for this precious, scarce resource making us unable to attend to the conversation?

The plate would be handed around. We'd take one, and wait. The grownups would keep talking. One of them would lean forward to take another biscuit, and then another. Finally there was only one left.

"Can I have another biscuit?" I'd pipe up, in last-chance desperation.

"See if anyone else wants it first."

So it had to be offered around the whole group, and usually (my cheek twitches as I write it) someone would say, "Thank you" and take it, and my heart would sink in my chest, the keenest disappointment of my very sheltered life.

You'll be detecting that I'm not quite over this memory. Ah well...

My point is, many of us have a sense that if we want something, and we get it, we are taking it from someone else.

The flip side is, if someone else gets something we want, we resent it, because we feel they have somehow taken it from us.

In this world of plentiful resources, neither of these things is true. Allow yourself to desire the things you desire – there is enough for everyone. Be happy for people who achieve your dreams ahead of you – they haven't taken from you, they have shown what is possible.

If you want something, want it full out; admit it to yourself and revel in it. Believe that what benefits you also benefits others, that more for you means more for everyone, more joy, more love, more of everything. This will allow you to fully appreciate the things you achieve, the things you receive, and to be generous at the same time.

(If you want to try this out, my good friend Stuart Fleming and I have put together a five minute guided visualisation. Search on YouTube for "Jennifer Manson visualization", watch it, then take note of how life unfolds...)

And on the other side, if you really don't want something, no matter how desirable it may seem to others, allow yourself to not want it, not strive for it, and put your energy into your more personal, individual dreams.

What doesn't need doing?

Celia Lashlie, in her book *He'll Be Okay*, talks about one of the reasons many teenage boys leave their assignments till the last minute: the world might end between now and when it's due, and in that case the effort would have been wasted.

I love this, and the idea encapsulated in it: some of the things we do simply don't need doing – we could not do them and it wouldn't make any difference at all.

Sometimes things that matter in the short term don't matter in the long term. J.K. Rowling says, "People very often say to me, 'How did you do it? How did you raise a baby and write a book?' and the answer is, I didn't do housework for four years."

In the long term, what is most important?

Sometimes things that sort of need doing might still be better not done. Reports that are written need to be reviewed and proofread and then read by the end audience. Sometimes, what is in the report is not critically important, and the time that goes into producing and reading it could be used better by all concerned.

So how do we know whether it needs to be done or not? Again, intuition tells us. It gives us the content and timing of our lives. The question is not, "Is this worth doing?" but "What is the best thing I could be doing with my time, right now?" It's a matter of prioritising, every moment, the things that are most important.

When I look back over the last few years at what has been important in my own life, it is my books that stand out. Once I acknowledged how important it was for me to write, I knew I had to do it, come what may.

At the time when I began writing in earnest, life was full. I was running two businesses, one full time, as well as loving to spend time with my two teenaged children.

Still, I made time to write, and in the end, once I honoured that calling, the time required was short: forty hours for the first draft of each book, and about the same for each edit – hardly any time at all, in the wider scheme of life flowing by.

I know, too, that once I was writing, following that dream, I was happier, more energised, more effective in everything I did.

As well as the books, my relationships are a high priority: spending time with my family, friends, and the people I've met – invaluable time, especially when we're talking about our hopes and dreams...

When my children were small and I wanted to spend time with them, playing with their toys, reading them stories, as well as creating a satisfying life for myself, I only did housework before 9 a.m. This was brilliant, focused my mind, helped me prioritise and move fast, getting things done in lightning time.

It was also good for the children, for their independence, since they got ready for school at their own speed, while I was busy, rather than tapping my foot, waiting, or stepping in and doing things for them that they could do very well for themselves.

EASY

It's amazing how much we can get done if we just open our minds to the possibility that things might be much, much, much easier than they seem.

Knowing when I'm finished

One day I was driving back from a client meeting knowing I had a newspaper deadline for the next morning. I had an idea for the story, but that was all. I also knew that I needed to be at school to pick up my daughter in 45 minutes, and that I wanted to spend time with her between pick up and dinner, because what's the point of having children if you don't have time to enjoy them?

Right. Forty minutes. Could I get the article done in that time? I was sitting at the traffic lights just near my house. I knew the phase of them, so I could confidently close my eyes for a few seconds and quickly perform a self-hypnosis to help me with my day. "Unconscious mind, please assist me to write the article in the time I have, and to know when I am finished."

I added that last bit because of my known tendency to check and double check my work, to go back and rethink it. With less than forty minutes available there wouldn't be time for that.

When I looked up at the clock a while later, having written, proofread and emailed a 750-word article, I saw that only thirty minutes had gone by. I had ten minutes left over to relax before I needed to get back in the car again.

The long-term effects of that self-hypnosis were even more startling. The "know when I am finished" part of it had been installed in me permanently, and now often when I am nearing the end of a task, a curious feeling will come over me, an irresistible sense of slowing to a halt.

If I'm writing, as in this book, chapter by chapter, or shorter articles or blogs, at a certain time I feel my hands lifting. My fingers come up off the keyboard; my left wrist, which habitually rests on my laptop to hold it steady as I type, comes clear of contact with the metal, and I know, with absolute certainty, that I am done.

If you're someone who second guesses yourself and your work, perhaps with perfectionist tendencies, you can imagine what a difference this makes. Somewhere deep inside, I know I'm finished, which means I am satisfied, sure, complete.

This thing in itself was a novel experience – but no more. Completion, satisfaction, and wildly enhanced effectiveness followed permanently and irrevocably from ten seconds with my eyes closed at the traffic lights not far from my home.

EASY

Five dream goals

One of the things I had on my list of five dream goals – a list I wrote when I was following Fiona Harrold's book *Be Your Own Life Coach* – was to renovate a house.

Through my years doing staging I saw lots of opportunities for profit through light renovation, many of which I realised for my clients by making the house they owned look its best for the market.

Then one day I decided to take the plunge. I had a contact at a network group who did house finding for people, so I set him on the case to search for just my kind of bargain. I knew what I was looking for: something sound but a bit tired. We looked at a couple of houses, I refined my brief, and the next week I made an offer on an investment of my own.

In the spirit of this book, rather than reinvent this content, here are the two articles I wrote for the Christchurch *Press* newspaper at this time, which detail the experience.

Looking for a place to renovate

Article reproduced from the Press *newspaper "at home" supplement October 2009.*

It has long been a dream of mine to renovate a property, and when I met Peter Barker, the Property Hunter, who specialises in finding property to specification, it seemed fated: the time was now.

Renovating a home can be a wonderful creative project. Not for me, however, the Herculean task of rewiring, re-plumbing, large scale building – I wanted a project where everything I did made a visible difference.

That being the case, what was I looking for? I started by thinking about where the biggest difference can be made.

Interior colour

Warm, light neutrals increase sense of space, reflection of light through the house and sense of warmth. If a house has cold or dark colours in the interior, simply repainting can take us a long way.

Light

Increasing natural light by pulling back window treatments and removing net curtains makes instant impact. Replacing dark or bold coloured curtains with light colours allows light from outside freer access to the interior.

Adding good artificial light is useful to supplement natural light – halogen spots, multi-bulb fittings, wall lights and freestanding lamps all add to the whole.

Bathroom and kitchen

These may benefit from greater investment. New flooring and fittings and a coat of paint in the bathroom can add immediate luxury to a house where this room has previously not been the best feature.

In the kitchen it is sometimes possible to update by simply recoating cupboard doors and drawer fronts and changing handles. Replacing appliances may provide the lift required, or we might decide to go for a total refit.

Furniture, art and mirrors

Here again, the difference made can be magical. Mirrors can double the sense of space in a room and increase light. Pictures with perspective such as large scale landscapes give the feeling of looking into the distance, making rooms feel larger, and well placed furniture creates easy flow.

Working within a visual theme of colour, texture and style of furniture and accessories creates a sense of unity and harmony, and overcomes many quirks and idiosyncrasies of architecture.

Exterior painting

A freshly painted house looks and feels well cared for. Outside, the range of shades which look good is wider – there is a current fashion for mid to dark charcoals, greys and browns as well as the traditional light neutrals. My preference is for natural, neutral shades and toning – usually lighter – window and door surrounds.

Landscaping

Depending on how long you plan to keep the property, landscaping can be approached in various ways. Landscape expert Jo Steele suggests planning the structural elements first – where the largest trees/plants will go – and planting these as soon as possible to achieve maximum growth in the time. In-fill planting can come afterwards.

For instant results, investing in larger trees and instant lawn can add huge value to a property in the space of a few days.

Outdoor spaces can be defined further with outdoor furniture – a park bench at the edge of a lawn or outdoor dining suite to draw attention to a pleasant paved area.

The Hunt

Having discussed these various aspects with Peter, the hunt began. We refined our search after seeing and discussing a few properties in the first week, and in the second week, he came up with gold.

Stay tuned for the next instalment!

Diary of a Renovation

Article reproduced from The Press *newspaper "at home" supplement November 2009.*

Following on from last month's article "Looking for a place to renovate" the renovation is now complete. Here's how it all happened.

Day 1: Tuesday

The painter starts. I have done some cleaning over the weekend prior, washing down the doors and skirtings which are still in good condition and don't need painting.

The paint colour looks great. As painting progresses it becomes clear that the carpet, which looked okay before, will need to be replaced. I am going on holiday tomorrow, so I need to choose carpet before I go.

The floor sanding expert comes and discovers that while there are good boards in most of the house, the kitchen/dining area floor is chipboard and hardboard. This means we will need to lay new vinyl rather than have polished wood, so there is another decision to be made before departing at 1 p.m. tomorrow.

Talked to landscaper on the phone. He is going to try to get here tomorrow morning to discuss what needs to be done outside.

Have decided a heat pump is essential. Getting quotes from two companies.

Day 2: Wednesday

Painting continues. I have chosen carpet and wood-look vinyl (still have that vision of wooden floor in my head.) Carpet is scheduled to be laid next Thursday and the vinyl needs to go down first – that means sweet-talking the vinyl company into some fast work, as the floor needs to be stripped and sanded before the vinyl can be laid.

Landscaper is tied up on another job and won't make it before I leave. He is a contact through a good friend so I ask him to consult with her about what he will do. Landscaping scheduled for Wednesday and Thursday next week, so I will be back by then anyway.

12.55 p.m. Leave on holiday five minutes ahead of schedule. Everything in capable hands of the trades people.

Days 3 and 4: Thursday and Friday – on holiday

Finalising quotes and scheduling work to be done next week: vinyl, carpet, heat pump and landscaping. Everyone is great about the short time-frame.

Enjoying the sunshine and sea views in Golden Bay.

Day 7: Monday

Back from holiday. In the meantime the painting has been finished, the new light fittings have been installed as well as the new heater and vanity unit in the bathroom. The deck has been water blasted and the outside on the front of the house washed.

All quiet.

Day 8: Tuesday

Vinyl measured and cut. Vinyl area floors cleared and sanded. Amazingly I get a call at 4 p.m. to say the vinyl laying is finished a day ahead of schedule.

Phone carpet company and heat pump installer to see if they want to come a day early – they both opt to stay with the Thursday installation.

Day 9: Wednesday

Landscapers working. We have decided to paint the main area of corrugated fencing, so that is being water blasted today. Garden looks hugely tidier by the end of the day.

All quiet inside.

Day 10: Thursday

Heat pump installed, finished 7 p.m.

Landscaping completed and fence painted. Garden rubbish cleared so you would never know it was there. Even to a non-gardener like me the garden looks fantastic!

Small hiccough with carpet, all laid except living room – carpet layer will be back tomorrow.

Day 11: Friday

Carpet finished – renovation feels complete. Still considering changing handles on kitchen cupboards and re-surfacing breakfast bar.

Days 12 and 13: Saturday and Sunday

Bring in furniture. And yes, once the furniture is in it is clear the kitchen handles need replacing and the bar needs resurfacing. I call the floor sander and ask him sweetly if he will do this small job. He says yes and schedules for next week.

Day 14: Monday

Windows cleaned.

Buy handles for kitchen and put them on. Discover the screws need to be shortened so call Anthony, the builder/painter, and ask him to do this one last thing, bring his hacksaw and cut forty screws to the right length and re-fit. He is an angel. At least the cupboards look all right from outside, so I can take photographs for the article!

So there it is, all done, except for the three days and three coats of polyurethane on the kitchen bar.

Thanks so much, guys, for all your fabulous work!

(Credits were given here to the local trades people involved.)

EASY

Fear of public speaking

The one problem with joining the National Speakers Association was that I would have to speak.

I was kind of fine speaking up in a meeting, and had NO trouble whatsoever one to one, in fact (as mentioned earlier, and to misquote Shrek) it was getting me to shut up that was the problem there. But getting up on stage, without a REALLY good reason... that was a different thing altogether.

Especially when it came to getting up on stage in front of a room full of professional speakers. They are the most generous people in the world, but really? Can you imagine?

In the spirit of doing the thing I feared most (more about that in the next chapter) I volunteered for the five-minute speaking competition. Wow! What a disaster! I don't mean a disaster like a flood or an earthquake, but as far as something can be bad in a nice room, in a nice part of town, with only kind, supportive people present, it was bad.

I don't remember much at all about the five minutes; for most of the time I was unconscious. Goodness knows what I said.

The feedback I got afterwards was that it would be better if I didn't read out my speeches; but I didn't have it written down.

Where to go from there?

Well, I worked out a couple of things. The next time I spoke in the competition, the following year, I set myself one objective: to stay conscious through the five minutes, so I could at least see the audience, and remember what had happened.

As it happened, just that thing was enough to resolve my abject terror for good. It seems that it was the going unconscious bit that was at the heart of the issue. Whatever I could see, I could face and conquer. You see, I really am brave, after all.

The other thing was, I worked out what would help my fluency. In between these two events, I'd delivered some other content at National Speakers, content I knew much better, based around my work, and I found this much, much easier.

I knew the subject, and I was confident speaking about it one to one, but that didn't completely explain why it was so much better in the context of standing up and delivering it.

What I worked out was that fluency in conversation, for me, translates directly into fluency on the stage. I had said this stuff so many times one to one, with the opportunity to watch the listener, adapt what I was saying according to the expression on their face, work out the ways of saying things that were immediately clear, and where I needed to change things.

After having done that many, many times, I knew what to say, my delivery was honed; I just needed to transfer that to the stage, and have a one-on-one conversation with lots of people at the same time.

So that's how I began preparing any new content for public speaking: I'd call up a couple of friends and ask if I could talk to them about this random subject for a while, until I got good at it. They were surprised, usually, but I have gorgeous, generous friends, so they very kindly went along.

Combining that with staying conscious, my presence on stage relaxed and improved, to the point that now, once I get there (there are still major jitters beforehand) I'm almost comfortable.

The thing I feared most

I don't know if the two things coincided, but I'm guessing they probably did. Like millions of other people, I read a book by Susan Jeffers called *Feel the Fear and Do It Anyway*; and (possibly less like millions of other people) I went on a facing-my-fears bender, taking myself on every morning, and doing the thing I feared most.

I don't know if you've ever tried it, asking yourself the question, "Out of the things I know would be good for me to do, what's the thing I fear most?"

If you've done it you'll recognise the sense of plummeting in the abdomen, the almost audible reaction: "Oh, no, not that." There's not even an exclamation point, because of the resistance that instantly forms, and also the leaden sense of dread; because at this point, it's happening, you can't avoid it. Not once you've been that honest.

So every day, I asked myself the question, "What's the thing I fear most?" and that's the thing I did first, initially with jerky run-at-it-and-stop hesitation, and then each day more easily, more quickly, with growing confidence.

And then, the miracle happened. One morning, when I asked myself that question, there was nothing. Of all the dragons in the den, there were none left – I had slain them all. Wow, what a moment! I bobbed to the ceiling and floated there for at least a day.

The habit has stayed with me, but now I don't have to wait for morning. As soon as something occurs to me that fits those criteria – good to do, and scares me deeply – that's the thing I do immediately. That's assuming the timing is right (more on this later).

Since that time, it must have been five or six years ago, there has only been one instance of putting something off. Since we're here, I'll tell you the story – it's a nice one.

STORIES FROM AN EFFORTLESSLY CREATED LIFE

Making that call

When my children were small, I went a little bit crazy. I'm a person who likes to do things, likes to create things with lasting value. I have ambition (shhh, whisper it, actually huge ambition) to achieve something in the world.

So while I loved my children, loved spending time with them, knew it was worthwhile to be there and teach them when they were small, it wasn't quite enough for me, and I was always irrepressibly looking for more.

Through that time, there were some children's stories that kept me sane, and many of them were written by New Zealand author Margaret Mahy – stories of visions and dreams, of people being true to their deep, real selves; stories told with humour and love.

They meant so much to me, these books: *Keeping House; The Three-Legged Cat; The Man Whose Mother Was a*

Pirate (one of my favourites); *The World's Highest Tray Cloth*.

I wanted to thank her personally, and once we moved back to Christchurch in 2003, I knew she lived just over the hill from us. Goodness knows why, but physical proximity somehow made the possibility seem easier, closer, more real.

I got her phone number through a beautifully coincidental sequence of events, which, to protect my sources, I will not reveal. I got her phone number; and then I hesitated.

That's how I knew how important it was to me – by that point I didn't hesitate over anything, not if it was out of fear, and that's what this was.

I had some natural delicacy about invading her privacy, but I knew I would be respectful, kind, grateful and brief; and I knew, for me, as a writer, I was always glad to hear such things. So it wasn't that that was holding me back.

There was an uncomfortable pause.

Finally, two days later I made the call. We had a brief chat, I thanked her for saving my life and my sanity, and for the joy she had brought to me, my children and countless others.

She thanked me for having called, and we said goodbye – a small moment for her, perhaps, but a big thing for me, to acknowledge one of my heroes.

If you haven't read her children's stories, do. They're all about people living their dreams, listening to their hearts. This woman is a national and international treasure.

EASY

Maybe it isn't time

Once I got to the point of knowing when something scared me, I discovered another thing about apparent procrastination: sometimes it isn't procrastination; sometimes it just isn't the right time.

Now that I instantly recognise the feeling of sinking dread that tells me something scary is coming that I will definitely do, I also notice the times when I'm not doing something, and there isn't that feeling attached. "That's interesting," I think, as I observe this phenomenon, "I wonder why I'm not doing that."

A simple example of this happened around the time I was leaving New Zealand to move to France. I had decided to close my staging business down rather than sell it against a backdrop of earthquakes and uncertainty in the property market, and I was selling and giving away everything associated with it, a refreshing process of letting things go.

The business had a website, and around five months after I began, a magazine started up in New Zealand with a very similar name. A year or two later they asked if they could buy my web address, but since by that time there were about 500 real estate agents who had my flier with that address on it, I said, "No".

Now, however, I didn't need it any more, and I knew a simple phone call would make them happy and bring me a few hundred dollars.

So why wasn't I making the call?

Now, here's one of the instances where the sceptical will say it was just coincidence. Maybe. I know that for a month or two I observed myself not making the call – no emotion, no resistance, just not doing it.

Then one day, with no prior sense of it, I found the phone in my hand, and my fingers tapping out their number.

Nick answered, I explained why I was calling, and here's what he said: "That's great. I'm just leaving the airport, heading into town. I'll be passing your house in five minutes. Why don't I drop in and we'll sort it all out?"

Two minutes earlier he'd have been in a meeting; two minutes later and he'd have been in his car and not taken the call.

Coincidence, maybe, but the timing worked really nicely for me.

EASY

STORIES FROM AN EFFORTLESSLY CREATED LIFE

Finding Lucy

We arrived in France and I continued to write as I had in New Zealand, taking at least five minutes a day to reconnect with the current novel, and add to it.

Or, at least, I did that for a while. I also set up a couple of clear days to edit the next book, and I came at that as I always did, with conviction and certainty of getting a good edit done in a couple of days.

Then things started to go wrong. The cat got sick and I didn't have a car to take him to the vet, which meant a disrupted day. I got sick, which was unheard of. Then a third thing happened, and I began to get the message it wasn't time for me to finish this particular book.

There's a danger here, a balance to be found between persevering come what may, and listening to what our environment is telling us. I was so used to the timing and process of my writing that I had continued to push the normal schedule when in fact my gut was saying "Stop. Not now."

"So what do I do, then?" I asked, once I finally got the message.

"There's nothing to do. Do nothing."

So against my inclination I did just that – in between the normal functions of everyday life, travelling in a new country and enjoying the scenery, I lay on the sofa and wondered what I was going to do next.

This wore thin after a while, and I railed against it, but once I settled down, considered the possibility that it was okay not to know, and allowed my mind to go quiet, inspiration came almost immediately.

I was reading a regular email I get, from Mike Dooley, *Notes from the Universe*, and an advertisement for a telesummit caught my eye. I hardly ever click on these things, but I clicked on the link and bought this one.

There were fourteen speakers and I listened to them all. The last was Lucy Whittington, who helps people find and do their Thing. Something in her message resonated deeply with me. I listened to her recording twice, filled out her web form to make contact, and the rest is history.

She became my first book client, my mentor, and introduced me directly or indirectly to almost the entire network I now have in the UK.

Being still, lying quiet, listening to my soul.

EASY

The body you want

I said I'd talk about how I lost weight – and more than that, how I transformed my body so that people tell me I look ten years younger.

It was something I'd been curious about for a long time. I had set the intention to be slim, lithe, beautiful, I had written it in my journal, but nothing was happening. I was okay, healthy, fine. But I didn't have the elegant figure I wanted.

As I sometimes do in this sort of situation, I had a conversation with my unconscious. I'm not sure how this works, but it always does. I formulate a question, and I wait for an answer, which always comes.

"Why haven't I got the body I keep asking for? I keep writing it: slim, lithe, beautiful. I keep playing the image of walking through Paris in a camel-coloured shift dress, moving beautifully. Why isn't it working?"

And the answer came: "You say that's what you want. You play that internal video. But actually, what you really want to do is lie on the sofa thinking about life. And you've got the perfect body for that."

My face twitched with annoyance. I knew it was true. I did love lying on the sofa thinking. I took a deep breath and put the question aside for a few days, letting it rest.

"Okay," I thought, "what is it? How are young bodies different from middle-aged ones?" I started observing, I watched out on films for figures that were what I aspired to. I'd heard friends complain about the inevitability of aging, and I didn't buy it. We have control over this stuff if we think we do.

The thing I noticed, more than anything else, that defined the difference, was in the length and slimness of the torso. I thought about that for a bit and realised that this was something I could influence with posture. If I pulled myself taller, not only did I proportionally lengthen, but I also got slimmer, doubling the effect.

I also noticed that young-looking people move more freely than older-looking people, regardless of actual age. So here's my formula for putting them together, and in seconds beginning a shift that snowballs into ever-increasing youth.

If this is something that interests you, try this: next time you are in a room with other people, pull yourself up taller and move more freely as you walk across the room.

That's it.

Immediately you look and feel younger and healthier. People begin to relate to you differently. Your unconscious absorbs the new way you are moving and begins to bring other aspects into line: your willingness to move, the food you choose to eat, and your confidence in attracting a mate, if this is what you want to do.

Which brings me to the other aspect of losing weight. I wasn't feeling particularly good, or particularly confident going out, either socially or to work, so I wrote the following in my journal: "I'd like a teacher to help me feel beautiful."

A few days after that, I was attending one of Lucy's events in England. It was there I found the people who were to teach me that lesson in a few minutes flat.

I had been talking to a good friend when suddenly there was a shift, I lost his attention, and I turned to see a beautiful woman had walked into the room. Although put out for a moment, I recovered quickly and thought about what I had seen. I realised I recognised that response, I'd experienced it myself when I was younger, although at the time I hadn't fully understood it.

"I'd like to experience that again," I thought, and as I sat next to Martha from JDV London at dinner, my mind was open to her assertion that whatever we want for our bodies is possible – we just have to create a space of safety for our bodies to change.

From that moment, my entire physiology altered. I wanted different foods, I moved differently, I thought about myself differently. Within seven weeks I had lost all the excess weight, and begun working with Martha to effortlessly tone and shape.

Three things: lengthening my torso and walking consciously, asking for a teacher to help me feel beautiful, and believing it was possible and easy; and it was.

EASY

Massive untapped potential – people want to make a difference

I had a nice moment a few weeks ago on a train. I got up as we neared my stop, and was reaching up to pull down my suitcase when one of a pair of rough-looking, rough-sounding men who were sitting near me got up from his seat, offered to help and lifted the case down for me.

"Thank you, that's so kind," I said, heartfelt. I smiled at him again as I got off the train, and through the exchange I felt his mood lift, his chest expand, puffing out with positive pride.

People want to make a difference. In his book *Punished by Rewards*, Alfie Kohn describes the difference between intrinsic and extrinsic motivation. To put his message in a nutshell, intrinsic motivation is much healthier for us.

When asked what motivates them and prodded a bit to go deep, people will come up with a list that includes enjoying what they do, a level of challenge, doing things they are good at, expressing themselves and being able to help others. People don't respond as well when they are rewarded for behaviour, because of the sense of being controlled that comes with it.

It's true for all of us, right? We love to help, to make a difference, without necessarily receiving something in return.

The startling contrast comes when people are asked what they think motivates others. The answer usually comes quickly: "Money". And then we stop and think. The disconnect is obvious. If we are motivated by all these good things, then other people probably are, too.

I was talking through my approach to people this morning with a good friend. This is something I like to do, to go round and round a subject in the process of working something out.

People often comment on the way I develop fast, deep relationships. I find out things about people that other people don't know. They tell me their deep, important stuff, often within minutes of us meeting, whether that's in person or on the phone or via Skype.

I have a few theories about why this happens. First, I'm a safe space for people to talk. They trust me, because it's safe to do so. I'm also deeply interested in who they are, what they have to say, and I draw from them three things that at a broad level encapsulate a lot of essential information: what they do, what they're great at, what they're passionate about. I love hearing that stuff, and I love sharing those things about me, too.

I have all the time in the world for this kind of conversation, and people sense that. The experience of someone with plenty of time for them is rare and precious and they open up within it.

The magical thing is that in fact, this approach is extremely time efficient. I make deep connections in one conversation, one phone call. We may talk for fifteen, twenty, forty five minutes, just once. It is amazing how much deep communication can happen within that sort of frame of time.

And sometimes, that's it. I may not speak to that person again. The connection is there, however, permanent, so that when our paths cross again – when we glimpse each other on Facebook, or in passing at an event – the deep sense of that conversation is reignited, brought to mind, replays itself again and again, as if it were a second conversation, and a third, and a fourth. The connection is reinforced through replay in memory, and we feel closer and closer over time.

The next thing that happens with those relationships comes back to intrinsic motivation – people love to help, and I know them well enough to know where they can help, with little effort, in a way that is self expression for them. When the opportunity arises, I can call on them.

It's about allowing them to make a difference without making it a trade. Sometimes it is paid work I am offering them, but not always; I don't always have to give them something equal in return, because often the knowledge of having helped is much more valuable.

I make things easy when I ask for a favour. I do whatever ground work I can, and always give an easy opt out in case it's something they don't want to do.

It's amazing, however, and beautiful, to see the joy with which people do help, almost every time I give them the opportunity. People love to help, and specifically they love to help me – I see it again and again, like with the guy on the train.

So why do these things happen to me? I don't think he would have got up for everyone. He wouldn't have been sure of his reception, of what the reaction might be.

I suspect there were subtle things that had gone on before that moment – a lack of fear, a lack of shrinking back, a staying open on my part when he got on the train and took his seat near mine. I might even have smiled at him. For some people that's not always the response they get. He knew well before that moment that he was safe with me.

He transformed for that moment into a knight in shining armour, and that would remain part of his repertoire of behaviour from that point on.

It's just about giving people space to be who they truly are, to trust the magic of intrinsic motivation.

A huge thank you to Alfie Kohn, for crystallising something I knew deep down, but hadn't been able to put into words before.

EASY

STORIES FROM AN EFFORTLESSLY CREATED LIFE

Knowing what not to do

One of the things I'm proudest of in raising my children is the ability we cultivated together in allowing them to say "no". When I think about it, it's something not many children are taught or allowed to do.

As I watched them grow, as I saw their brilliant capacity to know themselves, and know what was right for them, I began to run counter to many of the other mothers, and let them decide as much as possible for themselves.

The next step came for me when I was reading a story of three girls who had been kidnapped by a stranger. "How can we expect them to say no in that situation when we expect them to unthinkingly comply with other requests: running five laps around the playground for no obvious reason; looking at us when we talk to them; kissing Auntie Mabel on the cheek?" I asked.

"They know us," might be the answer, but is every adult they know equally trustworthy?

So I began standing up for my children's right to say "no". I believed it was more important to vary their learning than to do more of the same, so I told their teachers they wouldn't do homework. I told Jono's year three teacher she must not keep him in at break as punishment for not finishing his work.

Anything they felt strongly about I would defend their right not to do.

Sometimes this came with some concerns. Not wanting to give a speech at school, for example. Wouldn't it be good to push through that fear?

I decided in the end that the right to decide for themselves was more important.

Signing the note to opt out of the cross country was easier, for personal, historic and petty reasons of my own.

It's only now I see the full power of this. My children are strong in the face of their peers, and general expectation.

They choose what they will do, moving gracefully through life with economy of movement.

They follow their passions, leave aside the things that don't interest them, with the result that they are developing significant individual talents on their own.

I've learned from this, too, although I'm not as proficient at it yet as they. I must be getting fairly good at it, though; yesterday someone pointed it out as one of my strengths, and that knowing what not to do can be as important, define us as closely, as doing what we love.

EASY

STORIES FROM AN EFFORTLESSLY CREATED LIFE

Creating significant memories

Have you noticed that when you do something different, vary the everyday, you remember far more about it?

The way our brain works is to notice change, notice edges, and fill in the middle with more of the same. When we look at a wall, we see its edges and assume our reading of the rest. It's the same with time. In memory, a stretch of time without much variation contracts; a time of travel, of different experiences every day, expands in memory out of proportion to the time elapsed.

It takes very little effort to create valuable memories. Two of my best are the trips I made, one with each of my children, when each was twelve.

Jono and I travelled the Indian Pacific railway, from Perth to Sydney, an epic three-day journey through the

Australian desert, endless time, for talking or just for staring out the window dreaming.

With Alex it was the Ghan, from Adelaide to Darwin, a similar odyssey, stopping off to visit Uluru on the way, with all the out-of-time mysticism of that place.

It was at Uluru, too, that I read Douglas Adams' *The Salmon of Doubt*, the posthumous publication of his unpublished, and in some cases unfinished, manuscripts.

This, too, had a mystic, beyond-the-grave quality, leaving in its wake many long-term influences of thought: the deep analysis of the process of staring into a fire; the idea of following the random, in the form of thought, or a person, or a sequence of events – these have stayed with me far beyond the usual conscious awareness of the introduction of a new idea.

Three to four days in the company of a child-becoming-adult. Vivid in memory, now and for all time.

I'll sometimes vary this idea, expanding time through change of activity, and do the same thing as usual, but with a twist: a sales call with a novel theme, a surprising question to ask, or listening for different information.

Over the last few months I've been travelling my world, talking to familiar people, but having a different conversation. These talks run on a theme: the difference these people could make in the world.

I tell them what I see in them, the talents they possess, the influence they have, how they might use it.

It started as an individual compulsion, became a pattern, which I then began to understand. I don't think they or I will forget those conversations. Sometimes they took fifteen minutes, sometimes an hour; sometimes they happened on the sofa of their living room, sometimes at the dining table, sometimes walking on the beach.

We can create memory, create change, stretch time, just with a little unusual thought, just with the intention to do so. So why not? Let's do it.

EASY

A key to effectiveness

When our children were little, Paul and I had a debate that rested on the contrast between elapsed time and time input into a task.

He argued that it was more efficient to help the children get dressed; I argued that it was more efficient to let them do it themselves, and get on with something else in the meantime.

It depends on your criteria. If you have a deadline and need something done fast, elapsed time is the measure. If it's about long-term effectiveness, time of input is the key – the less time you input into something, the more you get done over time.

I use this fact over and over again in my work. In some cases it involves advance planning. In other cases, where there is no deadline, it just requires a big-picture awareness of where each project is at the current time; I can run many, many projects at a time, just pulling the strings and triggering the next part of the process. I have very little hands-on involvement at all.

There is almost always someone else who can do a task as well as I can – it's with the vision, the shape, the procession of events, that I can make the most difference. So that's what I do.

Some of it does go better with me directly involved. Because I have trained myself to be a responsive audience, for book projects it is best that I interview my clients myself. Likewise, with some of the editing of my own books and with my clients', I hold the whole thing in my head – shape and content – and can make tweaks to the order, to specific wording, bringing things back full circle and tying a theme back in. I love doing this, and it makes sense for me to do it.

Other things – transcribing, line editing, cover design, production – other people are better at these, so I just make sure I schedule them in, discuss things with those people at the appropriate time, inspire them with the larger vision and keep track of where they're at.

While they're working, I can be doing my thing with many other projects: inspiring, delegating, checking in; and expanding my network of inspired, inspiring people. That makes me smile, is exhilarating and relaxing at the same time, as I move into the space of getting to know someone, having all the time in the world to talk to them.

That's one of the things I love to do most; and then when it comes time that I need something new done, have something to delegate that I haven't before, I have a wealth of resource of people and talent at my fingertips. I know who to call on, who will love to do it, and who will adore being part of my creative world.

EASY

STORIES FROM AN EFFORTLESSLY CREATED LIFE

The efficiency of elegant design

My first career was in computer science and software design. In the heady days of the late 1980s I worked in Cambridge, in the software industry, in what was known then as Silicon Fen.

In those days before Windows we worked on an early windowing system; I wrote code for hypertext links before the Internet existed, and was part of a team planning cutting-edge user interface software for electron microscopes that had previously been controlled mechanically. One exciting project I had while on that team was translating gun-shot residue software used forensically in mafia-related criminal trials.

The thing I loved most when programming was the moment of conceiving a beautifully elegant solution to a software problem. Elegant code is far more efficient than the clunky kind – it's far easier to see that it will work, that it is written correctly; there is far less incidence of bugs.

At the level I worked, with brilliant, talented people, we all recognised elegance: it was the holy grail we all searched for, whatever we were doing. It might take a while of sitting back, considering, but it meant the work was done up front, when it was fun, rather than at the dull back end when we were up against a deadline and the code wasn't working. Effort at that end was thankless and boring; which gave us the perfect reason to seek and create works of art from the start.

The way I see it, every challenge, in every sphere of life is the same: there is always a simple, elegant solution. We often don't see it, because we often aren't looking, because the way we've always done things is fine.

My son Jono worked as a part-time dishwasher at a popular café in Christchurch. He never does things by rule or convention; he always works things out from first principles, making his own rules, his own way.

For the first few weeks after he started work, he'd occasionally have a breakage. This was normal, and no-one was much bothered or surprised; except Jono. Every time something got broken he would look at what happened, understand the contributing factors, and work out how to prevent it happening again.

After a while, the breakages dwindled, as each common cause was eradicated.

Perhaps we can apply this thought to the rest of our lives.

It depends on our tolerance, and our standards. What are we willing to accept as normal, acceptable, and where are we determined to reach for higher quality, lower margins of error, better return?

EASY

Governing assumptions

Our world is created by our expectations. Some people see it as normal to argue with their teenagers. Some people believe that it is normal for customers to complain about service, or to return a certain percentage of goods.

Some people believe 10% profit, or return on investment, is normal for a healthy business; for some it is 50%. Some people could aim for 20% growth in turnover, but not 200%. Some people believe that $50,000 is a good income, and some believe they couldn't survive on less than ten times that much.

Some people believe that their friends will betray them. Some people believe they can trust and their trust will be honoured. Some people believe life is easy, and some people believe life is hard.

In each of these cases, the beliefs largely dictate the truth, the facts, the outcome; so I began to wonder, is there a way to identify someone's governing assumption, and if so, is there a way to take them past it, to a place where it ceases to operate, and they are free to create a new world, for themselves and those around them?

I wondered what would happen if we got them to bypass that thing that governs their growth. "If you were to have achieved that 200% increase, what would change, what would be different in your world?"

It can be a bit of a mind-bend. To go beyond that place, which looks like fixed reality, can take a moment, because the brain hasn't gone there before. There can be a strong experience of gaping, of "uuuuum"; but then the machinery starts turning, the cogs start meshing, new possibilities become visible, then possible, and then sometimes move towards being probable, or even certain.

Once the mind has gone there, it can never go back. Once you've imagined beyond the constraints you hadn't thought to question, the box is open, thoughts run free.

The key is to work it out: what is your governing assumption? What is the idea that you consider so much absolute reality that you don't even see it; not that you hadn't thought to go beyond it, but that in your world there was no beyond?

A clue is in where you spend your thinking time. Once you're on track, once the fire-fighting of immediate emergencies is done, what do you think about? What are the challenges that occupy your mind? If it's how to get more customers, take a step up and out. Imagine a world where you had as many customers as you can handle, where you have expanded capacity and are far, far beyond the world you now inhabit.

Now take a look around. What is different? What is the same? What do you like, and what is less appealing? Spend some time here, answer some questions, take a look at what the current challenges are in this new reality.

And now step back, into your present world. Do those big questions look different? Do you have new insights into where the new customers might come from, or how many there might be?

EASY

STORIES FROM AN EFFORTLESSLY CREATED LIFE

Going into the future and bringing back certainty

When I started my furniture rental/home staging business, it involved a large investment. Thirteen house lots of furniture, with art, accessories, mirrors, lamps, was a big outlay, at least for me.

I had a loan covering the bits of the expenditure that hadn't been paid from cash flow on the initial hire, and although I paid what I could, when I could, a few years into the business that loan was still there, in the background – driving me crazy, actually. I hated owing money.

So I decided I wanted to pay it off, and I set myself an initial goal of $10,000 – no deadline, just a clear, tangible amount to pay off that would make me happy, or so I thought.

Sometimes the goals we set for ourselves are beyond our current experience. It is useful to imagine ourselves beyond that finish line, but if we haven't been there before, that isn't always easy to do. We don't know what it will feel like. We don't know how life will be.

It was a little bit like that with this particular goal. Money goals are prone to this "can't imagine it" symptom, because they're not really tangible, it's hard to get excited about them in this dry form; so in this situation I asked myself, "How can I make this real; how can I see past the achievement and feel how it will be?"

I decided on a couple of things I could do. One was that I had been wanting to buy a Nespresso machine, so that when we went to my parents-in-law's beach house we could have good, fresh espresso. Once I'd paid off that $10,000, I decided, I'd get myself a Nespresso machine.

There was also a juice bar I loved, where the orange juice had so much vitamin C that it would almost knock you off your chair. The rest of the celebration plan was to go to the juice bar, order a juice, and sit there drinking it, knowing I had paid off that part of my loan.

I vividly imagined both of these things, in a process I now call going into the future and bringing back certainty. I sat in those experiences as if I were physically there – and maybe, in some unknown sense, I was.

In two weeks, I had reached the sum. I put it in the bank, went and bought the Nespresso machine, went to the juice bar. Drinking the juice was a weird experience. Here I was, as I had imagined, sitting here knowing I had achieved what I said I would. But I felt weird. It had worked, but it felt uncomfortable... More on that in the next chapter.

For now, the point is, I couldn't imagine moving money from one account to another, because I couldn't get a handle on any emotion, any real experience. I could imagine buying a coffee machine, drinking orange juice, however; so that's what I did, and within a very short time, there I was.

The same thing happened with my books, my writing. I didn't know what it would feel like to be published, to have a book to sell, so I created an image for myself, a lived experience.

In the city art gallery in Christchurch is an air bridge, spanning the open atrium space between the two sides of the second storey. I went to this place – distinctive architectural features are often significant for me – and imagined myself standing here with my published novel, and recalling this moment of promise.

In fact, by the time I returned (and I have to confess, it was a friend who reminded me to do so) I had three novels. I took them each in turn, walked out onto the air bridge and felt the power: of promise, of returning, of imagination, and of being true to myself and my dreams.

In Paris, living my dream, and still not satisfied

"Okay, here I am, I've got it, the life I wanted. So why don't I feel any different?"

It was a very good moment, that moment, of realising all my dreams and not feeling satisfied, although it didn't feel like it at the time.

So where was I?

In Paris, in Café Deux Magots, on an autumn morning, drinking coffee, writing in my journal, with my beautiful family still asleep in the hotel. In a while I would take breakfast back to them, but for now, I had time to myself.

Later that day I would go out to research an article I had been commissioned to write for my newspaper back home, another dream realised; I'd wanted to be a writer since I was six, and here I was, being paid for it, in the most beautiful city in the world.

Still not satisfied.

Why?

For me, this was the start of a journey to a much deeper place, to a comfort within myself, inside myself, a realisation that my life was in my hands. It's not the place for that story, not quite yet. Maybe in the next book, maybe the one after. Or maybe it's in those countless other books by other authors that focus on this subject.

For now, let's just say this: until now, the outer circumstances had seemed to be what made the difference, what caused my dissatisfaction.

On this day, at this moment, looking through the window at the streets of Paris waking up for the day, with everything at my fingertips that I had ever wanted, I realised that wasn't it, that it wasn't the outer circumstances, that it was in my hands... that it was up to me.

Big results from small beginnings

I've mentioned before that I went a little bit nuts when my children were small, when I didn't have enough to do for me.

Once they started school, I wanted to go back to work. I looked around for programming jobs – even interviewed with Microsoft – and was offered one with a technical software company not too far from home. The only thing was, they wouldn't flex my hours, and I wanted, at least once or twice a week, to pick my children up from school.

So I kept looking, and finally was accepted as a lecturer in the computing department at Farnborough College of Technology.

"Just wait," they said. "We'll assign you some courses and let you know."

So I waited. And waited. Still nothing.

One day the frustration got to the point that I put on my best clothes and walked out the door of my apartment into the village, vowing to myself I wasn't coming back without a job.

For a while I'd had the idea of working for a real estate agent. There were some gorgeous houses in the area where we lived, rural Hampshire, with its architectural beauties, and I thought if I were taking people to do viewings I would get to see inside some of them. So I started with the real estate company that had its head office in our village. I walked in and asked if they ever needed someone to show the houses when the agents were busy, and offered myself.

The woman at reception looked up curiously. She was thirtyish, capable, intelligent; more the executive PA type than a bored receptionist.

She said they didn't do exactly that, but that they needed someone to run the office on Sundays.

"But I don't have any experience."

"I'm sure you have lots of transferable skills. Go home and write a CV."

Buzzing with this encouragement, but still without a job, I kept walking. There was a "Saturday assistant required" sign in one of the antiques shops, so I went in and was given that job on the spot.

I wrote my CV for the estate agent, took it back that afternoon and got that job as well. So now I had two jobs, one on Saturdays and one on Sundays. That left me very little weekend time with my family, but how would I choose?

"I'll do them both for a while, and see which one I like best."

In fact I loved them both, regardless of the modest pay, and I did well, selling two houses one Sunday afternoon, and learning an enormous amount about furniture and placement of objects to best effect and, from Sally, who owned the antiques shop, about throwing oneself into life, trying things, just doing them, and if they didn't work out, trying again.

I kept both jobs until the year ended, with teaching jobs at two colleges and a school as well – a busy, productive and massively educational year.

At the end of the year, we decided to move back to New Zealand, and with the experience I had at the antiques shop and estate agent, two part-time, one-day-a-week jobs for just a year, I knew everything I needed to start my home staging company, and to make that service, that company, a success.

What I learned from the real estate company

In my work at the real estate company it wasn't long before I began to see patterns in the houses that sold, or didn't sell – if I liked a house, it would sell; if I didn't like it, it would sit around for a while.

Being the scientist I am, I began to ask myself what it was that made the difference. I started to turn up to viewings fifteen minutes early, armed with a clipboard and comprehensive checklist, and looked around the house, focusing on each detail in turn.

What were the colours? How much natural light was there? How easy was it to navigate the house? What were the views?

Very soon I knew what led me to like a house, and it was much more definable than I might have thought.

I also listened to what potential buyers were saying, and how they moved in the space. One afternoon, I took a couple through two houses with identical floor plans. After we came out they made this interesting observation: "We liked the big one, but we didn't like the small one."

I knew the two houses were structurally the same, so I went back and looked at them, to work out what it was that altered the impression of size and space.

That was when I came up with my internal assertion (not one I ever delivered to an owner – I was only the Sunday girl, it wasn't my place). That assertion was: "Give me half an hour and a rubbish bag, and I can get you £10,000 extra on the price of the house, and actually sell it."

Looking back it's easy to see how this experience, combined with my deeper understanding of the feel of a property, would naturally lead to a career of setting up houses for sale.

What I learned from the antiques shop

At the antiques shop I was mostly employed just to work the till, but when the shop wasn't busy, and at the start and end of the day, I had other duties – some prescribed by the owner, some invented by me to keep me busy and engaged.

I wound the grandfather clocks, of which there was a roomful. I dusted and arranged the objects, and in the afternoons, when we usually had two staff on, I would sometimes be allowed to polish furniture – it was an absolute joy to learn each intricate corner of these beautiful pieces, as I applied the wax and then polished; intimate, feature by feature, until I knew each tiny detail.

As I worked with the antiques, both larger pieces of furniture and smaller decorative items, I developed an appreciation and feel for quality, for the different types of wood, and I also learned about visibility according to placement.

I'd put an object out, something I thought would sell, and it wouldn't. Then I'd move it to another position and it would sell the same day.

What was happening here?

I spent time considering this, worked out how our eyes move in a space, from point to point to point rather than sweeping evenly, and developed the theory of view lines that became the cornerstone of arranging houses for sale.

Here I also developed my theory of theming: that when a number of objects of similar colour and shape are grouped together, they read visually as one larger object. In staging, I used this idea to work with the objects already in the house, simply by rearranging and grouping, and also to simplify the visual detail so buyers remembered what they needed to about the house.

This knowledge had another minor but quite fun effect, on a day that otherwise could have been tedious: the day when I volunteered to help out at my children's primary school fair.

I was assigned to the bric-a-brac room, a place where many, many unwanted items, donated by hundreds of parents, were collected to be sold, or more likely not, to the same hundreds of parents who would traipse through during the day of the fair.

I walked in and looked around, and for want of something more interesting to do, I began collecting all the blue glass objects, cleared a small round table, and arranged them into a pleasing composition: taller at the back, smaller at the front.

The effect was striking. When the fair organiser came through her attention was caught by this group, bold amid the random chaos.

"Who did that?"

Before the fair had even opened, I had been promoted to the most prestigious role of the day: selling the large items of furniture, in pride of place in the school hall.

Robert McKee says there's no such thing as undiscovered genius, and apparently this is true in minor situations as well as major ones.

EASY

Controlling the out breath, relaxing on the in breath

Stellar trumpeter James Morrison says (and I'm paraphrasing wildly, apologies, James) that with breathing, most of us have things backwards. When we are asked to relax, we relax on the out breath, slumping down into a slouch, and trying to feel better from this position.

It works much better if we control the out breath and allow our bodies to breathe in naturally once we are empty of air. It's the way we are designed. The in breath happens beautifully, elegantly, inflating us to perfect posture, and leaving us lightly ready for anything.

It's obvious how this principle would work for playing the trumpet – beautiful control of the flow of notes, followed by instinctively healthy refilling – and it occurs to me to follow it through as a metaphor for life.

What are we giving out? What are we creating? Maslow identifies self-actualisation as the highest human need. We are not expressed by what we own, by what we accumulate, but by who we are, and from there, what we do, what we create.

The lower-level needs encourage us to search for input, not output. We think first about what we need to draw in: food, water, warmth, clothing; and sometimes, once those basic needs are met, we forget to turn around the process, we continue to try to draw in, rather than reaching the peak of healthy consumption and beginning to give out, beginning the exhale.

As with the body breathing, I find things come naturally when I am focused on what I give out, trusting the things I need to come in once I relax. When I know that I want to create something – it might be a story, or an experience – and I know I need resources in order to do that, my own personal history tells me the resources come easily in that context.

When I think I am in need, or might be in need, and look for the resources in isolation, or in advance, I have personally found it more of a struggle.

I see this around me, for example in friends searching for clients, to fuel their businesses, so they can fund their lives.

I prefer to come at it from the opposite direction. What do I want to do in the world? What do I want for my clients? What do I hope to give them? In this view, I usually don't have to go looking. Those clients, and the resources to serve them, appear to come looking for me.

EASY

Easy friendships

I have lots of friends, and for most of my life friendships have been easy for me.

There were a couple of moments in my twenties, however, where there was a little glitch, a little crisis of confidence; where I noticed that my friends had not been calling me, and I wondered if they were really interested, if they really liked me at all.

It was when I looked back over my history that I realised what was happening. Over my life it has usually been me who initiates social contact. It's usually me who makes the call, issues the invitation, sets things off.

At the times when I lost confidence, I was going through low phases, perhaps even depression, and I had stopped being the initiator, stopped making the calls.

For a little while after I noticed my friends weren't calling, I pushed things the other way, waited for them to make contact, got grumpy. When that didn't work, I started to think a little differently, a little more objectively.

"I like it when people call me," I reasoned, "so possibly, even probably, they like it when I call them."

I knew intuitively this was true. You can almost always tell from someone's voice if they are pleased to hear from you; and even if you're not sure, there are ways to check.

I also realised it gave me lots of freedom. If this was the way to go, it meant I could choose my friends, developing relationships with people I thought were cool. I could also effortlessly let go of the ones who drained me: if they called me, I was fine to spend time with them; but I knew they mostly wouldn't call, and those less desirable relationships would just fade away.

With all this in mind, I developed a clear strategy: I would choose the people I wanted to spend time with, and I would phone them up and invite them to do things – go out, come to dinner, talk on the phone. Then I'd listen to how they responded, how keen they were.

If they sounded positive, I'd suggest we set a time. If they leaped at that and did so, that was another step. If they were vague, non-committal, I'd leave it up to them to make contact again.

If, once we'd made an arrangement, they cancelled, I'd listen for their intention to reschedule. If that was missing, once again, I'd leave it up to them to make contact again.

These weren't hard and fast rules. I allowed for exceptional circumstances, and if I really wanted to spend time with someone, I'd leave it a decent interval and try again.

A few strikes and they were out, however; not from any judgement or fixed rule, but just working on the probability that I wasn't high on their priorities, or they weren't getting as much out of the relationship as me.

Over the years this has worked brilliantly for me. I have a huge close network, perhaps 400 people I could pick up the phone to at any moment. They might be surprised to hear from me – I don't keep up with 400 on a weekly basis – but mixed in with the surprise would be delight, and if they happened to have ten minutes to spare, we'd have an enjoyable catch up, reconnect, and leave the call feeling great.

Of course, there are closer and less close friendships. I value my very close friends extremely highly. I'm so grateful for the huge depth they add to my life.

Just recently, however, I'm wondering if there is another level to this: another level of connection and love and communication that is possible. Perhaps if I can see myself more clearly, trust myself and my friends more fully, be more open, more confident in myself, there is the opportunity of an even richer dimension, to those friendships, and to life.

Sustained extreme happiness

There's one more chapter I want to add before the end. It doesn't quite come into the category of making life easy, but it seems valuable for making life worthwhile.

The last few months have been rough ones for me. That thing I alluded to about adding unnecessary complexity to my relationships and emotions has been playing out on a massive scale.

Now, I know that I create whatever I want in life; I choose how I feel, how I respond to the things that happen around me, the circumstances of my life. So for a long time I asked myself: why would I choose grief? Why would I choose pain when I could choose happiness and peace? I know they exist; I know I could create them. So why not?

But somehow, the idea of "happiness" just didn't attract me. After the intensity of the everyday experience I was creating with my grief, how could mere happiness compare?

In common human experience, there are two things we associate with vivid happiness: new love and new babies. All other cheerful circumstances tend to deliver a much milder form. Nothing special. Nothing wildly exciting. And wildly exciting was what I craved.

Then I stopped myself. I recognised a semantic pattern, a resignation to something just because it was common in the status quo. I was assuming that just because sustained extreme happiness was not common in the world, I could not create it. But of course I could.

So here I am, having created the idea of sustained extreme happiness. So far, most people I've told about it have responded with scepticism. There's the caution of someone confronted with mania, fearing the depression that traditionally follows.

But why shouldn't I create this? We see prolonged grief all the time. I myself have lived it, brilliantly, for months on end. Why not flip the coin, live the other side? The intensity is possible, we all know that; it's just the flavour that would be different.

Having seen the vision, I'm certain it's possible. Having chosen it for myself, and, by contagion, for the people around me, I am sure it's on its way. There are clear moments of it already, glimpses of how it looks in reality, how it feels, how it is.

I'm eager to see the form it takes in the longer term, the circumstances of life that form around the central emotional experience. Life is already pretty good here: close relationships, physical expression, beautiful environment, work I love, plenty of time and money, and vibrant good health.

What more is possible? Watch this space.

EASY

Making projects easy

Making projects easy for me is about looking for ways to streamline the process, and then streamlining the search for an easier way.

I create with my words, speaking the possibility of something and knowing with absolute certainty that it is, that it already exists – somewhere in the future if not right here, right now. I feel it flow from my fingertips with the joy of creation.

I create an image, and see and feel the result, and I don't have to consciously think or plan my actions; I find myself moving, taking the actions that will bring about the result, often in a surprising and exciting way.

It's about creating something from nothing, an idea springing forth from the deep part of me that knows my life path, my direction and purpose; I accept that it is possible and go looking for it.

It is always there, ready for us to notice, to capture, appreciate and nurture into existence.

Trust your gut, your intuition, with the little things at first, and then the bigger ones. You'll find that bigger gets bigger and bigger as you go, until you've reached a place you may have thought of, but never thought you could reach; and then beyond that, to things you never dreamed possible.

Consider, if the project you thought would be your life's work could be done in ten months, or eight months, or six, or two, and easily delegated, what would you do then?

~~~~~~~~~~

If you have enjoyed

Easy

Stories from an
effortlessly created life

please email jennifer@jennifermanson.co.nz
to join my mailing list and receive information
about further publications, or see

www.jennifermanson.co.nz or
www.theflowwriter.com.

I welcome your feedback.

Please post your review on Amazon and
connect with me on Facebook

Facebook.com/theflowwriter

With my very great thanks,

Jennifer.

Made in the USA
Charleston, SC
07 March 2014